G. E. Brown BA

Brodie's Notes on George Orwell's

Nineteen Eighty-Four

Pan Books London and Sydney

First published 1977 by Pan Books Ltd,
Cavaye Place, London SW10 9PG

      6   7   8   9

© G. E. Brown 1977

ISBN 0 330 50064 3

Printed and bound in Great Britain by
Richard Clay (The Chaucer Press) Ltd, Bungay, Suffolk

Contents

Page references in these Notes are to the Penguin edition of *Nineteen Eighty-Four*, but references are usually given to particular parts and chapters, so that the Notes may be used with any edition of the novel.

To the student

A close reading of the set book is the student's primary task. These Notes will help to increase your understanding and appreciation of the work, and to stimulate *your own* thinking about it: *they are in no way intended as a substitute* for a thorough knowledge of the work.

The author and his work

'As to a pseudonym, a name I always use when tramping, etc, is P. S.
Burton, but if you don't think this sounds a probable kind of name,
what about
Kenneth Miles,
George Orwell,
H. Lewis Allways.
I rather favour George Orwell.'

The above quotation from a letter written in November 1932
to Leonard Moore, the literary agent, saw the birth of 'George
Orwell', which was the pen-name of Eric Blair. At the time the
letter was written Blair was awaiting the publication of his first
book, *Down and Out in Paris and London*, and because he felt the
nature of its subject matter might be embarrassing to his
family, he had decided to have it published under a pseudonym. All his books were published under the name of
George Orwell, a name which combines, as Anthony Powell
has pointed out, 'the most characteristically English Christian
name' and the name of a river in Suffolk, a county well known
to Eric Blair, since his parents lived for some time in the town
of Southwold. After 1932 Orwell continued to be known as
Blair to many of his friends, but as he became better established in the literary world so the number of his acquaintances
increased and many of them knew him only as George Orwell.
As time went by he took to signing even personal letters as
George Orwell, but he never took the name officially by deed
poll. In this section of the book I shall refer to him as Orwell.

He was born in India on 25 June 1903, the second child of
the marriage between Richard Walmesley Blair and Ida
Limouzin. Richard Blair was the son of a clergyman who had
begun his career in India, and he himself entered the colonial
service when it was time to choose a career. He joined the

Opium Department of the Indian government in 1875 and retired from government service in 1912. Ida Limouzin was several years younger than Richard Blair and had a French father and an English mother. In 1907 Richard Blair took his family back to England on leave and, as his wife was expecting a third child when his leave came to an end, he returned to India alone. Mrs Blair and her two children were established in a house in Henley-on-Thames and were not to see Richard Blair until he returned to England upon his retirement, at which time Orwell was eight years old.

At just about the time of his father's return to England, Orwell was sent away to preparatory school. It has been argued that he always felt a sense of rejection from the family because of this, and there can be no doubt that he disliked intensely his time at St Cyprian's, Eastbourne. Much later (in 1952) he was to publish a lengthy account of his prep-school days, 'Such, Such, Were the Joys', and one critic has even gone so far as to put forward the view that the squalor of many of the settings of *Nineteen Eighty-Four*, and the sense of fear of betrayal which is central to the novel, can be traced back to Orwell's days at St Cyprian's.

From St Cyprian's, after a brief spell at Wellington College, Orwell went on to Eton where he was a scholar from 1917 to 1921. Later he was to write: 'I did no work there and learned very little, and I don't feel that Eton has been much of a formative influence in my life.' Nevertheless, he received a good education at Eton and took part in sporting events, including the famous Wall Game. Orwell felt himself to be inferior to many of his contemporaries at school because his family had to make sacrifices to maintain him at Eton, depending as they did on his father's not very lavish pension. Undoubtedly this feeling of inferiority (the validity of which has been denied by several who knew Orwell at the time) was to have a great influence on his later life, and cause him to try to break away from the middle class background into which he had been born.

Accordingly, it is not surprising to find Orwell opting out of the customary sequel to being a member of College at Eton, that is, going on to university. He realized that he would have to win a scholarship to support himself at university, and decided against trying to do this. Instead he took examinations to enter the Indian Imperial Police, coming seventh in the list of those who passed. In October 1922 he set sail for Burma, where he was to remain until 1927.

Orwell was a perfectly competent police officer in Burma, but, as he writes, he gave up the life 'partly because the climate had ruined my health, partly because I already had vague ideas of writing books, but mainly because I could not go on any longer serving an imperialism which I had come to regard as very largely a racket.' He was, however, to use his Burmese experiences later in essays such as 'A Hanging' and 'Shooting an Elephant', and, of course, in his novel *Burmese Days*, which he wrote in 1933.

On his return from Burma Orwell began systematically trying to get to know the life of the lower classes from the inside. Between 1927 and 1929 he spent time in the East End of London and in working-class districts of Paris, living in cheap lodging houses and often wearing clothes bought in second-hand shops. In the latter part of 1929 he worked as a dishwasher and kitchen porter in a Paris luxury hotel and restaurant. During these years he was writing without any great success, but his experiences formed the subject matter of his first book, *Down and Out in Paris and London*, which was published by Victor Gollancz after being turned down by Jonathan Cape and Faber and Faber.

Before the book was published, Orwell had begun work on his first novel, *Burmese Days*, which was actually his third book to be published in England, as his publishers insisted on alterations in it for fear of a libel action. Orwell worked as a teacher in small private schools during 1932 and 1933, thereby gaining material for his second novel, *A Clergyman's Daughter*, which was published in 1935. In *A Clergyman's Daughter* Orwell also draws on his experiences as a tramp and a hop-picker, and in this novel he utilizes material from *Hop-Picking*, a journal which he wrote in 1931.

Orwell's next novel was *Keep the Aspidistra Flying* (published 1936), which was partly based on his experiences as a part-time assistant in a bookshop in Hampstead where he worked for almost two years. Gradually he was becoming better known, and in addition to his novels he was writing articles and book reviews, which meant that by about 1935 he was able to live on what he gained from his writing. In 1936 he set up a small general store in Hertfordshire, writing to tell a friend that: 'If I do open it will be only for certain stated hours so as not to interfere with my work.'

That work was becoming more overtly political in tone at the time. In 1936 he was commissioned by Victor Gollancz to go to Lancashire during the Depression to report on the situation there. The result was *The Road to Wigan Pier*, published in 1937. Orwell himself described the book as 'too fragmentary and, on the surface, not very left-wing'. In fact, when it was published, Gollancz felt it necessary to write a special introduction to counteract what Jenni Calder has called Orwell's 'biting if rather crude attack on the left-wing intellectuals of the time, who took up theoretical postures without coming close to the facts that inspired them'.

In July 1936 the Spanish Civil War began. Orwell, who had recently married, left for Spain where in December he enlisted in a Marxist militia group known as the POUM. He spent January to May 1937 fighting against the Fascist forces in Spain, but on 20 May he was severely wounded in Barcelona when he was shot through the throat by a sniper. In June 1937 he wrote to Cyril Connolly describing his wounding, 'which of course ought to have killed me but has merely given me nervous pains in the right arm and robbed me of most of my voice'. He later regained the use of his voice, but his experience left him with a deep mistrust of Stalinist Communism as he had seen it operating in Spain. He returned to England determined to tell the truth as he saw it about events in Spain. However, Victor Gollancz refused to consider publishing anything critical of the Communists, and Orwell was forced to change publishers for *Homage to Catalonia* (1938). Fredric Warburg, who brought out the book, later became the publisher of all Orwell's work, but he remained with Gollancz for the publication of *Coming Up For Air* (1939).

Prior to the publication of *Homage to Catalonia*, Orwell, who had not enjoyed good health since his schooldays, had spent some time in a sanatorium suffering from tuberculosis in one lung. A gift of £300 from L. H. Myers, the novelist, enabled him to spend the winter of 1938–9 in the warm climate of Morocco. During this period he wrote his sketch, 'Marrakech', published at Christmas 1939.

When war began in September 1939 Orwell tried hard to enlist in the army, but was rejected because of his medical history. So he joined the Home Guard and continued with his journalism, principally for *Tribune* and *Time and Tide*. He also brought out a short book, *The Lion and the Unicorn* (1941). In August 1941 Orwell joined the BBC as a Talks Assistant in the Indian Section of the Eastern Service, later becoming a Talks Producer. His experiences at the BBC between 1941 and 1943, together with the knowledge he gained of the workings of the Ministry of Information, left him with great misgivings about the morality of propaganda even when it was being used with the best motives. He felt that any connection with propaganda corrupted those who used it, and he was later to make use of many of his experiences of these years when he came to write *Nineteen Eighty-Four*.

Throughout his period at the BBC Orwell continued to write

for a variety of newspapers and magazines. In November 1943 he resigned from the BBC to become literary editor of *Tribune*. He began to write his satirical fable *Animal Farm* towards the end of 1943.

Animal Farm was rejected by a large number of publishers when it was completed, because it was highly critical of Russia, at that time a close ally of Britain. Orwell at one time considered bringing it out himself as a pamphlet, but it was finally accepted for publication by Secker and Warburg. It was published in 1945 in Britain and in America the following year, and sold extremely well. For the first time Orwell was freed from financial cares. However, a few months before the book's publication his wife died while undergoing an operation.

In 1946 Orwell's *Critical Essays* were published. In July 1945 he had revealed to Leonard Moore that he had begun to write the novel that was to be *Nineteen Eighty-Four*, and that he did not expect to finish it until 1947. He continued to write for newspapers and magazines and spent much of his time with his young adopted son in a cottage that he had rented on the island of Jura in the Hebrides. Gradually his health began to deteriorate, but he completed his novel, which was published in June 1947. By this time he had experienced several spells in hospital because of his tuberculosis. In September 1949 Orwell's condition caused him to be transferred from a sanatorium in Gloucestershire to University College Hospital, London. In October 1949 he married again in a ceremony performed at the hospital. He felt that he was getting better, although he was still very weak and ill. In October he wrote that his doctor had suggested that he 'should spend the worst of the winter abroad, probably in France'. However, in January 1950 Orwell died in hospital at the age of forty-six.

The book

The title

In a letter to his publisher, F. J. Warburg, dated 22 October 1948, Orwell stated that he first had the idea for *Nineteen Eighty-Four* in 1943. He continued, 'I think it is a good idea but the execution would have been better if I had not written it under the influence of TB. I haven't definitely fixed on the title but I am hesitating between "Nineteen Eighty-Four" and "The Last Man in Europe".'

He appears to have had two reasons for finally choosing the former title. First he wanted readers to be aware that his nightmare vision could become reality within their lifetime if they did not exercise vigilance. He therefore set his book a mere thirty-five years in the future, and, it would seem, obtained his title by reversing the final two digits of the year in which the book was completed (i.e. 19*48* became 19*84*). Secondly, Orwell may have had in mind a footnote in Jack London's *The Iron Heel* concerning the building of the two cities of Asgard and Ardis, which reads: 'Ardis was completed in AD 1942, while Asgard was not completed until AD *1984* [my italics]. It was fifty-two years in the building, during which time a permanent army of half a million serfs was employed. At times these numbers swelled to over a million – without any account being taken of the hundreds of thousands of the labour castes and the artists.'

Towards *Nineteen Eighty-Four*

'I belong to the Left and must work inside it, much as I hate Russian totalitarianism and its poisonous influence in this country.'

(Orwell, in a letter to the Duchess of Atholl, dated 15 November 1945)

'Every line of serious work that I have written since 1936 has been *written, directly or indirectly, against* totalitarianism and *for* democratic Socialism, as I understand it.'

(from 'Why I Write', 1946)

These two quotations, together with statements that he made shortly after the publication of *Nineteen Eighty-Four*, make it clear that Orwell continued to support the cause of Socialism while being intensely concerned about the dangers of totalitarianism which, he felt, '*if not fought against*, could triumph anywhere'. He has described how it was the Spanish Civil War and other events of the mid-Thirties that gave him a true idea of where he stood politically, but ironically, it was his experiences in Spain (described in *Homage to Catalonia*) that caused him to consider fully the dangers of totalitarianism and led him to write the two books in which he makes his fullest attacks on totalitarian regimes – *Animal Farm* and *Nineteen Eighty-Four*. Throughout the 1940s he continued to criticize totalitarianism in his letters, broadcasts and journalism. In particular he was appalled at the way in which objective reporting of facts was impossible in a totalitarian state and by the fact that 'Totalitarianism [had] abolished freedom of thought to an extent unheard of in any previous age.'

In 1941 Orwell delivered a broadcast, 'Literature and Totalitarianism', in which he points out that 'If totalitarianism becomes world-wide and permanent, what we have known as literature must come to an end.' He describes the way in which the totalitarian state 'tries, at any rate, to control the thoughts and emotions of its subjects at least as completely as it controls their actions', and, anticipating *Nineteen Eighty-Four*, he indicates how it

'sets up unquestionable dogmas, and . . . alters them from day to day . . . It declares itself infallible, and at the same time it attacks the very concept of objective truth.'

Orwell goes on to point out that 'writing is largely a matter of feeling, which cannot always be controlled from outside' and that 'writing of any consequence can only be produced when a man *feels* the truth of what he is saying'. He concludes his talk by calling on those who value literature to resist totalitarianism.

Orwell's later essay, 'Looking Back on the Spanish War' (1942), contains much that is central to his thinking, and points forward to Winston's job of rewriting past events in *Nineteen Eighty-Four*. In this essay Orwell describes the ways in which newspaper reports bore no relation to the facts in the Spanish War:

'I saw great battles reported where there had been no fighting, and complete silence where hundreds of men had been killed. I saw troops who had fought bravely denounced as cowards and traitors, and others who had never seen a shot fired hailed as the heroes of imaginary victories . . . I saw, in fact, history being written not in terms of what happened but of what ought to have happened according to various "party lines".'

He goes on to describe Fascist propaganda about the war in Spain, with its cynical disregard of the facts, saying that he finds it frightening 'because it often gives me the feeling that the very concept of objective truth is fading out of the world'. Later he writes of the ways in which totalitarian governments were busily destroying any body of neutral facts on which impartial judgements could be made, and he states that

'The implied objective . . . is a nightmare world in which the Leader, or some ruling clique, controls not only the future but *the past*. If the Leader says of such and such an event, "It never happened" – well, it never happened. If he says that two and two are five – well, two and two are five.'

The parallels with *Nineteen Eighty-Four* are obvious.

Orwell was to return to the idea of the manipulation of factual information on many occasions, perhaps most tellingly in his essay 'The Prevention of Literature' (1945). Here he refers to the organized lying that 'is something integral to totalitarianism, something that would still continue even if concentration camps and secret police forces had ceased to be necessary', and he goes on to reiterate the point that he had made in his broadcast of 1941, that 'Totalitarianism demands . . . the continuous alteration of the past, and in the long run probably demands a disbelief in the very existence of objective truth.' Orwell considers that 'Totalitarianism . . . does not so much promise an age of faith as an age of schizophrenia', since 'its doctrines are not only unchallengeable but also unstable. They have to be accepted on pain of damnation, but on the other hand they are always liable to be altered at a moment's notice.' He was later to demonstrate this satirically in *Nineteen Eighty-Four* when, on the sixth day of Hate Week, the crowd is thrown into confusion when 'at just this moment it [was] announced that Oceania was not after all at war with Eurasia. Oceania was at war with Eastasia. Eurasia was an ally.' (Part Two, Chapter 9, p.147.)

Orwell's concern with totalitarianism was not confined to his fear of the ways in which such a system imposed limitations on what it was permissible to think. An examination of his journalism also reveals how frequently he returned to the problem of the power structure that might follow the Second World War. In several essays he postulates a very similar set-up to that which exists in *Nineteen Eighty-Four* with its world divided into three super-states locked in never-ending combat, with only the alliances changing from time to time. Much of Orwell's thinking in this direction was influenced by the writings of an American professor of philosophy, James Burnham, and in particular *The Managerial Revolution*.

In 1944, writing in *Tribune*, Orwell includes Burnham in a list of those who refuse 'to recognize a difference between the Nazi and Soviet regimes', and hold that 'all Fascists and

Communists are aiming at approximately the same thing'. In 1945 he writes,

'Already, quite visibly and more or less with the acquiescence of all of us, the world is splitting up into the two or three huge super-states forecast in James Burnham's *Managerial Revolution*. One cannot draw their exact boundaries as yet, but one can see more or less what areas they will comprise. And if the world does settle down into this pattern, it is likely that these vast states will be permanently at war with one another, though it will not necessarily be a very intensive or bloody kind of war.'

In 1946 Orwell wrote an essay which was later reprinted as a pamphlet entitled *James Burnham and the Managerial Revolution*. Once again he takes up Burnham's forecast of 'great super-states grouped round the main industrial centres in Europe, Asia and America', and he foreshadows *Nineteen Eighty-Four* when he writes that, in Burnham's view, 'Internally, each society will be hierarchical, with an aristocracy of talent at the top and a mass of semi-slaves at the bottom.'

In his essay, 'Burnham's View of the Contemporary World Struggle' (1947), Orwell deals with the development of Burnham's views in *The Struggle for the World*, but the essay is chiefly of interest for Orwell's recapitulation of Burnham's thesis in *The Managerial Revolution*, which he describes as 'a good description of what is actually happening in various parts of the world, i.e. the growth of societies neither capitalist nor Socialist, and organized more or less on the lines of a caste system.' We have to wait until Orwell's article 'Toward European Unity', published in *Partisan Review* in 1947, for his own forecast of how the world would develop. However, once again Burnham's influence is evident.

In his article he outlines three possibilities, after making the stark statement, 'If I were a bookmaker, simply calculating the probabilities and leaving my own wishes out of account, I would give odds against the survival of civilization within the next few hundred years.' He chose the third possibility as his model for the situation which exists in *Nineteen Eighty-Four*. The first two possibilities seen by Orwell were: (1) 'That the Americans will decide to use the atomic bomb while they have it and the Russians haven't'; and (2) 'That the present "cold war" will continue until the USSR, and several other countries, have atomic bombs as well.' A holocaust will then follow, destroying industrial civilization throughout the world.

The third possibility envisaged by Orwell is that 'the fear inspired by the atomic bomb and other weapons yet to come will be so great that everyone will refrain from using them.' He calls this 'the worst possibility of all', foreseeing 'the division of the world among two or three vast super-states unable to conquer one another and unable to be overthrown by any internal rebellion'. Orwell forecasts a hierarchical structure within each super-state, 'with a semi-divine caste at the top and outright slavery at the bottom', and he suggests that the necessary psychological atmosphere would be maintained in each state 'by complete severance from the outer world, and by a continuous phony war against rival states'. Orwell then puts forward the view that only by making democratic Socialism work throughout some large area, as in 'a Socialist United States of Europe', could a viable model of an alternative kind of society be put up which 'could be made a reality in short enough time to prevent the dropping of the atom bombs'. He recognizes the difficulties standing in the way of establishing a western European union. In the absence of such a political federation, he was to endeavour to point out the dangers inherent in the postwar situation by writing *Nineteen Eighty-Four*.

Literary influences and parallels

'My new book is a Utopia in the form of a novel. I ballsed it up rather, partly owing to being so ill while I was writing it, but I think some of the ideas in it might interest you.'

(Orwell, in a letter to Julian Symons, dated 4 February 1949)

Here Orwell acknowledges the influence of a type of writing in which he had shown great interest for several years before coming to write *Nineteen Eighty-Four*. Basically the type derives from *Utopia*, written in Latin by Sir Thomas More, first published in 1516 and translated into English in 1551, although writers earlier than More had imagined ideal societies, for example the ancient Greek philosopher Plato in his *Republic*. More's Utopia (the name means 'Nowhere') is an imaginary island where poverty and injustice do not exist, and religious toleration is practised. The name of More's political romance has since been used as a general term to describe other books which outline conditions in imaginary ideal states, for example William Morris's *News from Nowhere* (1890) and several of the works of H. G. Wells. In addition, it has sometimes been used incorrectly (as by Orwell himself in the letter quoted from above) as a label for books like *Nineteen Eighty-Four* in which far from ideal states are described. More correctly such works should be called *dystopias*.

Orwell's temperament and political convictions attracted him towards several noted examples of dystopia, and at intervals in his career he wrote about three of them in particular. These were Jonathan Swift's *Gulliver's Travels* (1726), Jack London's *The Iron Heel* (1907), and Yevgeny Zamyatin's *We* written in 1920, first published in 1924). Many of his comments on these books are of interest not only in their own right, but for the ways in which they point forward towards *Nineteen Eighty-Four*.

In 'Politics vs Literature: An Examination of *Gulliver's Travels*' (1946) Orwell draws our attention to certain aspects of language which obviously influenced him when he came to write *Nineteen Eighty-Four*. In Part IV of *Gulliver's Travels*, Gulliver, a ship's surgeon, is transported to a land ruled over by the Houyhnhnms, a race of horses endowed with the powers of reason and speech, and becomes the servant of one of them who treats him kindly, whereas other human beings are called Yahoos and are treated with contempt. When it becomes known that Gulliver and his master are friendly, the Houyhnhnm is exhorted to get rid of him. Orwell comments,

'(a Houyhnhnm, we are told, is never *compelled* to do anything, he is merely "exhorted" or "advised") . . . This illustrates very well the totalitarian tendency which is implicit in the anarchist or pacifist vision of society.'

He continues by describing the way in which public opinion can put a human being 'under continuous pressure to make him behave and think in exactly the same way as everyone else', and, returning to the Houyhnhnms, notes that 'they had apparently no word for "opinion" in their language, and in their conversations there was no "difference of sentiments". They had reached, in fact, the highest stage of totalitarian organization, the stage when conformity has become so general that there is no need for a police force.' While there is still a need for the Thought Police in *Nineteen Eighty-Four*, general conformity is the rule, and Orwell's statement regarding the absence of certain terms from the language of the Houyhnhnms prepares us for the reduction of vocabulary in Newspeak. As Orwell states in his appendix, 'The Principles of Newspeak', 'It was intended that when Newspeak had been adopted once and for all and Oldspeak forgotten, a heretical thought – that is, a thought diverging from the principles of Ingsoc – should be literally unthinkable, at least so far as thought is dependent on words.'

On several occasions in his journalism and essays, Orwell wrote about *The Iron Heel* (1907), a novel by the American writer Jack London (1876–1916), which he said 'has had the reputation of being an accurate forecast of the coming of Hitler', but his fullest comments about the book are to be found in an introduction he contributed to a selection of London's short stories which was published in 1946. I have already indicated that *The Iron Heel* may have been the source of the title of *Nineteen Eighty-Four*, and there is ample evidence that Orwell was influenced by London's novel, although in 1940 he called it 'hugely inferior' and 'clumsily written', and described its hero as 'a kind of human gramophone'. His introductory essay to the short stories contains much that is of interest because of the influence of *The Iron Heel* on *Nineteen Eighty-Four*, although Orwell's book develops in a very different way.

After making the point that Jack London's reputation took an upward bound after 1933 when *The Iron Heel* once more seemed to be of significance because of Hitler's rise to power in Germany, Orwell continues, '*The Iron Heel* is not a good book, and on the whole its predictions have not been borne out. Its dates and its geography are ridiculous, and London makes the mistake, which was usual at that time, of assuming that revolution would break out first in the highly industrialized countries.' Orwell goes on to describe how 'London imagines a proletarian revolution breaking out in the United States and being crushed, or partially crushed, by a counter-offensive of the capitalist class', and the way in which this is followed by 'a long period during which society is ruled over by a small group of tyrants known as the Oligarchs, who are served by a kind of SS known as the Mercenaries.' The parallels with *Nineteen Eighty-Four* are obvious. Winston rebels against the Party and throughout the novel hangs on to the belief that 'If there is hope, it lies in the proles', although O'Brien makes it clear to him that this is nonsense. The Oligarchs may be compared to the members of the Inner Party and the Mercenaries to the guards who assist them.

Other ways in which *The Iron Heel* influenced Orwell become apparent as we read further in his essay. He draws attention to the way in which London 'foresaw, for instance, that peculiar horror of totalitarian society, the way in which suspected enemies of the regime *simply disappear*.' Reading this, we are reminded of the disappearances of Winston's father, mother and sister, of the fact that the only person Julia 'had ever known who talked frequently of the days before the Revolution was a grandfather who had disappeared when she was eight' (Part Two, Chapter 3, p.107), and we recall the opening paragraph of Part Two, Chapter 5 when 'Syme had vanished'. The 'printed list of the members of the Chess Committee, of whom Syme had been one . . . looked almost exactly as it had looked before – nothing had been crossed out – but it was one name shorter. It was enough. Syme had ceased to exist: he had never existed.'

Orwell quotes at length a passage from *The Iron Heel* in which London analyses the mentality of the Oligarchs, emphasizing that, as a class, they 'believed that they alone maintained civilization . . . Without them, anarchy would reign and humanity would drop backward into the primitive night out of which it had so painfully emerged.' The imaginary author of London's book stresses that 'The great driving force of the Oligarchs is the belief that they are doing right.' Orwell remarks on what he then saw as London's understanding of the nature of a ruling class, but when he came to write *Nineteen Eighty-Four* he presented a blacker picture of the motives of the ruling group than London offered in *The Iron Heel*. In the Ministry of Love O'Brien asks Winston why the Party clings to power and receives the reply, 'You are ruling over us for our own good . . .' This is not the right answer, and Winston is punished for his failure to see that 'The Party seeks power entirely for its own sake. We are not interested in the good of others; we are interested solely in power.'

Other aspects of *The Iron Heel* may have influenced Orwell in *Nineteen Eighty-Four*, two positively and one negatively.

For example, the hero of *The Iron Heel* is Ernest Everhard, and the novel takes the form of a narrative by his wife, Avis, with the addition of footnotes supposedly written seven centuries later. The Everhard Manuscript, as it is called in the footnotes, breaks off abruptly in the middle of a sentence, and may have given Orwell the idea for the diary which Winston begins to keep in *Nineteen Eighty-Four*. The footnotes may have also suggested to Orwell the possibility of adding his appendix, 'The Principles of Newspeak', which is presented as though written by a narrator in future time after the conclusion of the action of *Nineteen Eighty-Four*.

Just as Orwell had offered a more depressing view than Jack London of the reasons for a ruling class wishing to remain in power, so the presentation of the hero figures in the two novels is very different. According to his wife, Ernest Everhard was 'a natural aristocrat . . . a superman, a blond beast such as Nietzsche has described, and in addition he was aflame with democracy.' She refers to him as 'my Eagle, beating with tireless wings the void, soaring towards what was ever his sun, the flaming ideal of human freedom', and describes him also as a great lover. Some critics have felt uneasy with Avis Everhard's over-emphatic hero-worship in *The Iron Heel*, and it is obvious that Orwell reacted against the portrayal of Everhard when he created Winston in *Nineteen Eighty-Four*. Winston is no 'Eagle'; he has a varicose ulcer and false teeth, and is even impotent when he first tries to make love to Julia. Orwell needed an ordinary man with human weaknesses and faults of character for the plot which he had in mind. The image he meant to leave his readers with in *Nineteen Eighty-Four* is that of Winston standing naked and broken before the three-sided mirror in the Ministry of Love, remembering O'Brien's statement, 'If you want a picture of the future, imagine a boot stamping on a human face for ever.'

In February 1944 Orwell wrote to Gleb Struve, a lecturer at

London University who had sent him a book he had written about Soviet Russian literature. In his letter Orwell refers to another novel that was to influence him when he came to write *Nineteen Eighty-Four* – *We*, by the Russian author Yevgeny Zamyatin (1884–1937). Orwell writes that he had not heard of *We* before reading about it in Struve's book, and continues, 'I am interested in that kind of book, and even keep making notes for one myself that may get written sooner or later.' In 1946 Orwell reviewed a French translation of *We* in *Tribune*. At that time the book was not available in English.

We is about a totalitarian society of the twenty-sixth century. In an introduction written for an English edition of 1970 Michael Glenny describes how *We* was circulated clandestinely in Russia in typescript form, but has never been published within the Soviet Union. The book was first published in America in 1924, but a Russian translation published in 1929 in Prague caused Zamyatin to be expelled from the Russian writers' federation, which effectively meant that he was unable to publish in newspapers or journals within Russia. Zamyatin applied to Stalin for permission to leave the country, and when this was granted settled in France in 1931.

From the time that he first heard of Zamyatin's novel until shortly before his death Orwell kept *We* in mind. In March 1949 he was writing to his publisher, Fredric Warburg, recommending *We* for re-issue in English, admitting that the book had faults, but calling it 'an interesting link in the chain of Utopia books'. Orwell goes on to suggest that Aldous Huxley's *Brave New World* 'must be plagiarized from it to some extent', and suggests that it is 'a good book in the same way as *The Iron Heel*, but better written'. Earlier, in 1948, he arranged to review an English translation of *We* for the *Times Literary Supplement*, but plans for an English edition fell through at that time. We therefore have to go back further, to Orwell's 1946 *Tribune* review of the novel, to find his fullest comments about *We*.

His review consists largely of outlining the plot of the novel and pointing out the ways in which Aldous Huxley's *Brave New World* resembles it. However, it is evident that many aspects of *We* influenced Orwell equally in writing *Nineteen Eighty-Four*. He describes how in Zamyatin's Utopia the inhabitants have lost their individuality so completely that they are known by numbers, how they wear identical uniforms and 'live in glass houses (this was written before television was invented), which enables the political police, known as the "Guardians", to supervise them more easily.' There is no marriage in Zamyatin's state, 'though sex life does not appear to be completely promiscuous'. These features were either taken over completely by Orwell in *Nineteen Eighty-four* or adapted slightly by him, as in his invention of the two-way telescreen for police supervision of the inhabitants of Oceania.

Orwell describes the plot of *We* as 'rather weak and episodic', and 'too complex to summarize', but he does refer to certain developments which have obvious parallels in his own novel. Zamyatin's narrator is D-503, a gifted engineer, who falls in love with I-330 (called E-330 in the 1970 English translation), 'a member of an underground resistance movement' who 'succeeds for a while in leading him into rebellion' against the Single State which 'is ruled over by a personage known as The Benefactor, who is annually re-elected by the entire population, the vote being always unanimous.' Finally D-503 is operated on by the authorities to eradicate his rebellion, and betrays his colleagues to the police. Sitting alongside The Benefactor in the Chamber of the Gas Bell Glass, D-503 watches I-330 being tortured before she is sent to be liquidated. Reading this we are reminded of Winston's cry in Room 101 – 'Do it to Julia!' Another significant point of resemblance between *We* and *Nineteen Eighty-Four* is the attitude adopted by each author to his dictator figure, although of course Big Brother never makes an appearance in Orwell's novel. Orwell praises *We* in his review for its 'intuitive grasp of the irrational side of totalitarianism – human sacrifice, cruelty as an end in itself, the worship of a Leader who is credited with divine attributes', all of which are to be found in his own book.

In addition to the three examples of dystopia which appear to have particularly influenced Orwell, he was also affected by a novel of a more realistic type when he came to write *Nineteen Eighty-Four*. This was *Darkness at Noon* (1940), by Arthur Koestler, the Hungarian-born author whose first two novels were written in German but first published in English translation. Koestler had been a member of the Communist Party when he was a journalist in Germany and he spent 1936 and 1937 in Spain reporting the Civil War. In 1938, disillusioned with Communism, he left the party. His novel *Darkness at Noon* is based on the Moscow trials of the 1930s, and tells the story of Nicolas Salmanovitch Rubashov, a fictitious leading figure of the Russian revolution who is thrown into prison and persuaded by his captors to confess to imaginary crimes against the state. Orwell was no doubt reminded of Rubashov's imprisonment and 'confession' when he invented Jones, Aaronson and Rutherford in *Nineteen Eighty-Four*, and certain details of Rubashov's interrogation are mirrored in Orwell's novel, in addition to the description of his execution by a revolver-shot in the back of the head while walking down a long corridor.

Themes

The main theme of *Nineteen Eighty-Four* concerns the limitations imposed on human freedom by a totalitarian regime. Orwell shows how such a regime can impose its will on its people by a sophisticated system of supervision and terror, involving the secret police, planted mirophones, and telescreens in public places and private homes. In addition to these instruments of the state's power, which are always there as reminders of the dangers of unorthodoxy, Orwell shows how the state has an even greater potential for imposing its authority by means of control of the media and manipulation of language. Not only are the powers of propaganda used to whip up enthusiasm for Big Brother and hatred for the chosen enemy of the moment, but by means of the efforts of the workers in the Ministry of Truth the past is rewritten so that Big Brother is shown to have always been right. In addition, the Party has decided to limit (and eventually eradicate) the possibilities of revolt against accepted ideas by the use of Newspeak. When Newspeak is finally perfected the language in which to express thoughts and opinions which run counter to the views of the Party will no longer exist, and the Party will be literally all-powerful.

Some critics have seen this theme of the limitations imposed by the Party on human freedom as having strong affinities with the authoritarian structure of the Roman Catholic Church. They equate the invisible Big Brother with God and see the members of the Inner Party as his priesthood. In this way it is possible to interpret O'Brien's concern that Winston should return to the Party's way of seeing things as the priest's desire for the conversion of one who has lapsed from the faith, and in support of this view we should remember the scene in O'Brien's flat in Part Two, Chapter 8, when O'Brien gives Winston and Julia wine to drink and hands each of them a flat white tablet to place on the tongue. The parallels with the Communion service are evident.

Connected with the main theme of the novel is the question of the survival of human love and aspiration in the face of overpowering odds. Orwell examines the question and seems to accept that characters such as Winston and Julia will try to work for their individual freedom in their own ways, as when Winston begins his diary and they succeed in engineering conditions in which to carry on their love affair. However, we learn later in the book that the Thought Police were always aware of their rebellion and were only waiting for the right moment to bring them in. It is in the sections set in the Ministry of Love that Orwell shows that he rejects the possibility of the human spirit rising above pain and privation. After a short while Winston 'hardly thought of Julia . . . He felt no love for her, and he hardly even wondered what was happening to her' (Part Three, Chapter 1, p.184). Eventually he is shown breaking down totally in Room 101 and shouting frantically, 'Do it to Julia! Do it to Julia! Not me! Julia! I don't care what you do to her' (Part Three, Chapter 5, p.230).

Orwell himself wrote that the novel would not have been so gloomy if he had not been so ill at the time that he was writing it. Certainly Winston's reactions to Room 101 and his remembered meeting with Julia in the Park (Part Three, Chapter 6, pp.233–5) are the most dispiriting sections of the book. One can only put forward the point that the history of religious and political movements is full of the records of people who did not call out for their pain to be transferred to someone else, but obviously *Nineteen Eighty-Four* would not make such an impact without the destruction of the love between Winston and Julia.

Structure

'I am not a real novelist anyway . . . One difficulty I have never solved is that one has masses of experience which one passionately wants to write about . . . and no way of using them up except by disguising them as a novel.'

(Orwell, in a letter to Julian Symons, dated 10 May 1948)

Orwell here reiterates a point he made frequently about his not being a real novelist. Early in his career as a writer he had been ready to be critical of his own fiction, and he later even went so far as to buy up copies of *A Clergyman's Daughter* when he found them in bookshops and destroy them, in addition to refusing permission for the book to be reprinted in his lifetime.

Nevertheless, he chose the novel form in which to communicate his ideas in *Nineteen Eighty-Four*, and was very aware of the care that he had taken in planning what he referred to as 'a novel about the future . . . in a sense a fantasy, but in the form of a naturalistic novel'. His American publishers asked him to alter and abbreviate the novel prior to publication, but he refused to do so on the grounds that 'It would alter the whole colour of the book and leave out a good deal that is essential.' In a letter to his literary agent Orwell writes,

'A book is built up as a balanced structure and one cannot simply remove large chunks here and there unless one is ready to recast the whole thing. In any case, merely to cut out the suggested chapters and abridge the passages from the "book within the book" would mean a lot of rewriting which I simply do not feel equal to at present.'

He concludes his letter by stating, '. . . I really cannot allow my work to be mucked about beyond a certain point, and I doubt whether it even pays in the long run.' So the book was published in the form that Orwell wanted, although its success as a novel has been questioned by certain writers, in particular because of the inclusion of the sections from Goldstein's supposed book, referred to by Orwell in the extract from the letter above, and the appendix on the principles of Newspeak. The arguments for and against the effectiveness of these two blocks of material within *Nineteen Eighty-Four* are dealt with towards the end of this section.

The structure of *Nineteen Eighty-Four* is a simple one, as was noted originally by Fredric Warburg in his report on the novel prior to recommending it for publication by Secker and Warburg. He details the breaking down of the novel into three sections as follows:

'Part One sets the scene . . . Part Two contains the plot, a very simple one . . . Part Three contains the torture, breakdown, and re-education of Winston Smith . . .'

In Part One Orwell concentrates on making us aware of the personality of Winston, the rebel against the Party system, and in so doing gives a detailed description of life in Oceania in 1984. We see Winston at home and at his work at the Ministry of Truth. The dreariness of life is stressed and the mechanics of the operation of the propaganda machine at the Ministry of Truth are described fully. By means of flashbacks within Winston's memory the early days of the Revolution are re-called, in addition to his own sexual, marital and family history. The different conditions in which the proles live are described, and we are introduced to 'the handful of characters who serve the plot, including Julia with whom Winston falls in love' (Warburg).

Part Two, which is chiefly concerned with the love affair between Winston and Julia, begins idyllically and ends in horror. Julia reveals her love to Winston and they overcome great obstacles in order to meet in the countryside and make love. At the end of Part Two they are brutally surprised within the room over Mr Charrington's shop, where they suppose themselves free to act as they choose. The plot is advanced in this section of the novel by the visit of Winston and Julia to O'Brien, whom they believe to be a fellow rebel against the Party. O'Brien arranges for Winston to receive a copy of Goldstein's book, which he begins to read in bed in the room he has rented for Julia and himself. Winston reads a lengthy section of Goldstein's book (which has in fact been partly written by O'Brien) aloud to Julia immediately prior to the invasion of the room by the Party guards.

In Part Three Winston passes through the process of rec-lamation by the Party, a process involving physical torture and humiliation, before he can accept the Party's way of seeing things. Orwell shows symbolically how Winston is ready to be re-educated by the contrast between the picture of him emaciated and stinking as he stands before the three-sided mirror when ordered to do so by O'Brien, and the figure he presents at the beginning of Chapter 4, bathed, wearing 'new underclothes and a clean suit of overalls', having had his varicose ulcer dressed with soothing ointment, and having been provided with 'a new set of dentures'. Nevertheless, before he can fully accept the Party view of things Winston has to be completely broken by the visit to Room 101, and is then released into the outside world.

Structurally, what follows refers back very effectively to earlier stages of the novel. Winston is now an habitual visitor to the Chestnut Tree Café, just as the discredited trio of revolutionaries, Jones, Aaronson and Rutherford, had been, whom Winston had recalled so vividly in Part One, Chapter 7. While sitting in the café Winston remembers a meeting with Julia which occurred after their release from the Ministry of Love. In contrast to the first occasions on which he had noticed her, Julia's waist has grown thick and stiff. Again, in contrast to the occasion of their first lovemaking, the weather is bitingly cold, the earth is like iron and the grass seems dead. The sadness of the scene is enhanced when we remember the descriptions of the dappled light and shade, the bluebells and the thrush singing in Part Two, Chapter 2. The actual novel ends in a way that forces us to recall its beginning. In the Chestnut Tree Café Winston hears the news from the tele-screen of Oceania's great victory over Eurasia. He looks up at a vast poster of the face of Big Brother on the wall. The caption now seems to indicate to him that Big Brother is watching over him benevolently. This is in striking contrast to the opening of the novel when the discontented Winston returns to his flat one lunchtime to begin his overt rebellion against the Party by starting a diary. On each landing as Winston climbs the stairs to his apartment a poster of Big Brother gazes from the wall. The picture of the enormous face is 'so contrived that the eyes follow you about when you move'. The sense of threat is evident.

In some of the individual notes later in this book I have

drawn attention to other structural devices used by Orwell to give a satisfying sense of shape to *Nineteen Eighty-Four*. However, it is necessary at this point to examine the two features of the novel which have caused some readers difficulty in regarding it as a satisfactory work of art – Goldstein's book and the appendix on the principles of Newspeak.　　•

Fredric Warburg, in his publisher's report on *Nineteen Eighty-Four*, was the first to draw attention to the fact that Goldstein's book 'can almost be read as an independent work', but he implies no criticism by this statement. Other writers have reacted strongly both for and against the inclusion of Goldstein's book within the novel. Robert A. Lee, in *Orwell's Fiction* (1969), points out that *Nineteen Eighty-Four* contains 'features which are, at the least, extraordinary to most conventional definitions of the novel: the appendix of "The Principles of Newspeak" and the long digression of Emmanuel Goldstein's (supposed) book, *The Theory and Practice of Oligarchical Collectivism*', but goes on to say that 'Orwell uses Goldstein's book to produce a highly effective dramatic moment within the plot'. Lee also states that the two supposed interpolations are skilfully 'assimilated into the fabric' of the novel.

For Keith Alldritt, however, the chapters quoted from Goldstein's book 'are of some interest as an essay on the possibilities of future history. But they do not allow themselves to be smoothly integrated into the development of the novel' (*The Making of George Orwell: An Essay in Literary History*, 1969). Alldritt agrees with those who have suggested that the extracts from Goldstein's book 'seem better suited to an appendix'.

Other writers disagree with views such as those expressed by Alldritt, and in support of the inclusion of the extracts from Goldstein's book go further than Robert A. Lee. Philip Rahv and William Steinhoff are two critics who have drawn attention to reasons for their inclusion subtler than those expressed by Lee.

Philip Rahv, in an article in *Partisan Review* (1949), stresses the parallels between Goldstein and Trotsky, whom he calls a 'useful scapegoat', and puts forward the view that 'The inserted chapters from Goldstein's imaginary book on *The Theory and Practice of Oligarchical Collectivism* are a wonderfully realized imitation not only of Trotsky's characteristic rhetoric but also of his mode and manner as a Marxist theoretician.' William Steinhoff, in *The Road to Nineteen Eighty-Four* (1975), suggests that the style and content of Goldstein's book are inspired by the writings of James Burnham, whose work I have discussed in another section of this book (Towards *Nineteen Eighty-Four*). In addition to the parallels with Burnham, Steinhoff propounds the interesting hypothesis that Goldstein's book is the Party's 'sacred book'. Steinhoff believes that three authoritarian ideologies are satirized in *Nineteen Eighty-Four* – Communist, Fascist and Roman Catholic. He writes that 'each group, from its beginning as a weak and despised sect, had its sacred book: *Das Kapital, Mein Kampf*, the Bible.' He goes on to suggest that it was therefore necessary for the Inner Party in Oceania to create another sacred book, 'just as it invented Emmanuel Goldstein'.

Whatever the individual reader's reaction to the inclusion of the lengthy extracts from Goldstein's book within the novel, few will dispute the point made by Lee that the book is used to produce a highly effective dramatic moment within the plot. In Part Two, Chapter 9, Winston is reading Goldstein's book aloud to Julia while they are in bed. Orwell shows the touch of an assured novelist when he has Winston break off reading just at the point when it seemed as if he would learn the answer to the question of the Party's real motive for seizing power. 'He had still, he reflected, not learned the ultimate secret. He understood *how*; he did not understand *why*' (p.173). Winston then falls asleep alongside Julia, and before he has an opportunity to continue reading the book they are captured by the Thought Police. Winston has to wait for the answer to his question until O'Brien reveals it in Part Three in the Ministry of Love.

The Appendix – *The Principles of Newspeak* – contains the fullest explanation of the principles of the language which the Party uses as one of its chief instruments of power, although in the main body of the novel Orwell has already shown the way in which the language operates in those sections where Winston is shown at his work and in the conversation between Winston and Syme in the canteen in Part One, Chapter 5. Robert A. Lee sees the Appendix as the most disturbing element in the novel because ' "The Principles of Newspeak" are described in the *past* tense. If we believe Orwell, we are past 1984 and closing in on 2050.' This is a point that has also been made by Howard Fink, in an article in *The Critical Survey* (Summer 1971). He draws attention to the fact that the mock-survey of the language of Oceania 'has been often misread as Orwell's comments in his own person', and goes on to detail the ways in which Orwell has parodied three particular books in constructing his own artificial language, Newspeak – C. K. Ogden's *Basic English* (1930), Lancelot Hogben's *Interglossa: A Draft of an Auxiliary for a Democratic World Order* (1943), and F. A. von Hayek's *The Road to Serfdom* (1944). The first two of these books are concerned with artificial languages which attracted attention during the Second World War because of their possibilities as means of international communication. Orwell himself was impressed by what Fink calls 'Hogben's purpose, to solve international discord by international communication' but came to see the dangers inherent in artificial languages which, by their nature, excluded the possibility 'of expressing fairly subtle meanings with the maximum of clarity'. F. A. von Hayek's book was 'a personal exposure of Fascist techniques in Germany and Italy' and Orwell, who reviewed it, took from it many ideas concerning propaganda and the destruction of meaning in language when he came to invent Newspeak.

Many of the more startling aspects of Newspeak are based on actual parallels with Basic English and Interglossa. Ogden was proud of the fact that he had managed to reduce the vocabulary of Basic English to 850 words while Hogben cut his list of necessary words to only 750. It is only a short step from such pruning of language to Syme's statement in Part One, Chapter 5:

'Don't you see that the whole aim of Newspeak is to narrow the range of thought? In the end we shall make thoughtcrime literally impossible, because there will be no words in which to express it. Every concept that can ever be needed, will be expressed by exactly one word, with its meaning rigidly defined and all its subsidiary meanings rubbed out and forgotten.'

Having read this passage again and pondered on its implications, we are forced to reconsider Lee's remark that *Nineteen Eighty-Four* contains features which are extraordinary to most conventional definitions of the novel, and recognize as he himself does later that 'The book . . . for all its coherence of structure, [is] thematically incomplete without the Appendix.'

Settings

The settings of *Nineteen Eighty-Four* are important for the way in which they conjure up particular atmospheres appropriate to what Orwell wishes to communicate. As I have pointed out elsewhere in this book, Orwell intended his novel to be a warning concerning what could happen if totalitarianism was allowed to develop unchecked, and he therefore set his novel not in the distant future but a mere thirty-five years after the date of publication. The book was published while the Second World War was still fresh in people's minds, and many of its results were still evident in physical form, as could be seen, for example, from the bombed sites in and around London. As a result, many of the individual features of the settings of *Nineteen*

Eighty-Four can be traced back to the England of 1939–45. I have mentioned some examples in individual notes later in the book, but it will be useful at this point to look closely at certain features of the settings of the novel.

At the beginning of the book Winston returns to his flat in Victory Mansions to begin his diary. Everything is squalid. The lift does not work and the hallway smells of boiled cabbage and old rag mats. The weather is bitingly cold and a swirl of gritty dust pursues Winston to the entrace to the flats. Inside everything is dreary, and from his window Winston can see vistas of rotting nineteenth-century houses and bombed sites covered with willow-herb. Everything reflects the frustration which Winston feels, and it is obvious that wartime England is mirrored in these descriptions. Turning to an article by Orwell published in *Tribune* on 9 February 1945 we find him writing: 'At this moment the block of flats I live in is partly uninhabitable: not because of enemy action, but because accumulations of snow have caused water to pour through the roof and bring down the plaster from the ceilings. It is taken for granted that this calamity will happen every time there is an exceptionally heavy fall of snow. For three days there was no water in the taps because the pipes were frozen: that, too, is a normal, almost yearly experience.' Evidently the squalor of life in Victory Mansions was similar to that experienced by Orwell in the Second World War.

Other settings in the early sections of *Nineteen Eighty-Four* are described in ways that both reflect what life was like in the Second World War and reinforce the feelings of frustration felt by Winston before he starts his love affair with Julia and begins to make progress (so he believes) in his revolt against the Party. For example, the Records Department at the Ministry of Truth is described in all its mechanical horror so that Winston and his fellow workers are made to appear like insignificant insects contributing their small quota to the life of the controlling power. In Part One, Chapter 5, Orwell goes further than this to emphasize the decline in the quality of life since the Party has taken over. The canteen where Winston meets Syme and Parsons resembles a British restaurant in the Second World War, but Orwell stresses all that is vile about it, from the greasy metal trays to the pannikins of pinkish-grey stew resembling vomit. The crowded restaurant and the deafening noise are emphasized, and the appearance of Parsons on the scene, reeking with stale sweat, adds to the unpleasantness. Everything about the atmosphere in the restaurant is appropriate to Winston's state of mind, and the chapter ends with the remaining tobacco falling frustratingly out of his cigarette when the whistle blows as a signal to return to work.

Winston has, however, begun his rebellion by starting the diary, and one day he finds himself in the prole area where he bought the book in which he intends to record his thoughts and experiences. The descriptions of the prole quarter are not very different from those of working-class areas Orwell would have known. He describes the ideal set up by the Party as 'something huge, terrible, and glittering' and contrasts it with the reality of 'decaying, dingy cities where underfed people shuffled to and fro in leaky shoes, in patched-up, nineteenth-century houses that smelt always of cabbage and bad lavatories.' Yet it is here that Winston finds his possibility of physical escape from Party supervision, in the room over Mr Charrington's shop.

Before taking the room from Mr Charrington, however, Winston starts his liaison with Julia. Significantly, he has dreamed of her before he speaks to her for the first time. In his dream the innocence of their love finds its physical manifestation in the Golden Country, where the natural world contrasts strikingly with the life of Victory Mansions and the Ministry of Truth. The warmth of the summer evening in Winston's dream is very different from the biting wind of the first pages of the novel.

When Winston and Julia reveal their love for one another

they have difficulty in finding a place to meet. Julia, however, has had previous love affairs and she and Winston meet in the countryside in a place known to her that resembles the Golden Country of his dreams. Here the quality of the natural world is used by Orwell to reinforce the genuine feeling that exists between the two lovers.

It is significant that the two occasions which Orwell describes on which Winston and Julia make love before they rent the room over Mr Charrington's shop take place in the open air. It is as though nature is giving a blessing to their union, although some might find it ominous that their second session of lovemaking takes place in 'the belfry of a ruinous church in an almost-deserted stretch of country where an atomic bomb had fallen thirty years earlier'. The meeting in the belfry occurs on a blazing afternoon, yet 'The air in the little square chamber above the bells was hot and stagnant, and smelt overpoweringly of pigeon-dung.'

After a while 'the temptation of having a hiding-place that was truly their own, indoors and near at hand' proves too much for Winston and Julia, and they take the room over the junk-shop. The room is rather seedy, but it has a homely quality about it. It resembles the kind of room that Orwell had written about earlier in his career in his essay 'Decline of the English Murder' (1946):

'It is Sunday afternoon, preferably before the war. The wife is already asleep in the armchair, and the children have been sent out for a nice long walk. You put your feet up on the sofa, settle your spectacles on your nose, and open the *News of the World*. Roast beef and Yorkshire, or roast pork and apple sauce, followed up by suet pudding and driven home, as it were, by a cup of mahogany-brown tea, have put you in just the right mood. Your pipe is drawing sweetly, the sofa cushions are soft underneath you, the fire is well alight, the air is warm and stagnant.'

Winston and Julia create a home for themselves in Mr Charrington's room, but are betrayed to the telescreen concealed behind the steel engraving of St Clement Dane's. In this way Winston's horror of rats, which is to break him in the Ministry of Love, is revealed to the Party.

Other settings in *Nineteen Eighty-Four* are less important in a symbolic way than those mentioned so far. O'Brien's luxury flat is a great contrast to Victory Mansions, but we have already learned from Julia that members of the Inner Party have the best of everything. When Winston is transported to the Ministry of Love the atmosphere is once more squalid, as it was in the lock-up where he had been taken immediately after his arrest. Once again, Orwell emphasizes those qualities that reflect Winston's being at a disadvantage. The female prisoner in Part Three, Chapter 1 vomits 'copiously on the floor', Winston has a dull pain in his belly and the lights are never turned out. Ampleforth is unshaven and has 'large, dirty toes . . . sticking out of the holes in his socks', while Parsons casts a longing glance at the lavatory pan, rips down his shorts and uses the lavatory 'loudly and abundantly. It then turned out that the plug was defective and the cell stank abominably for hours afterwards.' Everything combines to take away the dignity of the individual.

Other aspects of Orwell's descriptions of the settings in the Ministry of Love are important in so far as they reflect the stages of Winston's 'reintegration'. At first he is strapped down tightly during the interrogation by O'Brien (Part Three, Chapter 2, p.192), but gradually he is allowed to have his bonds a little looser (Part Three, Chapter 3, p.209). Eventually, after he has begun to make his effort to conform, his varicose ulcer is dressed with soothing ointment and he is given new dentures and clean clothes (Part Three, Chapter 4, p.220). Nevertheless, Winston is unable to hide his inner rebellion from O'Brien, and is sent to Room 101. 'The room where he had been interrogated by O'Brien was high up near the roof. This place was many metres underground, as deep down as it was possible to go.' The psychological implications are evident. In Room 101 Winston will look into his very soul.

After his release from the Ministry of Love Winston frequents the Chestnut Tree Café, significant as the meeting place of the 'traitors' Jones, Aaronson and Rutherford remembered by Winston earlier in the novel. The setting is dreary, the table tops dusty, and the flat oily smell of the Victory Gin is inextricably mixed up in Winston's mind with the smell of the rats in Room 101. However, the most striking setting mentioned in the final section of *Nineteen Eighty-Four* is the Park on the occasion remembered by Winston when he and Julia met after their release from prison. As I have pointed out in an earlier section ('Structure'), the contrasts between their meeting in the Park, and their meeting in the countryside on the occasion of their first lovemaking, are striking and poignant.

Symbolism

The novel as a whole lends itself to symbolic interpretation, and in previous sections such as that on 'Settings', as well as in some of the individual textual notes, I have drawn attention to examples of Orwell's use of symbolism. For example, it was not merely because Orwell wished to remind his readers of the Second World War that he described a landscape in which damaged houses and bombed sites were prominent. He obviously intended to convey by a kind of shorthand that the quality of life in Oceania was being eroded by the system of government. The use of imagery and symbol in this way colours one's whole view of the novel. However, it may be helpful to draw attention to two of the more striking symbols which are carefully interwoven by Orwell into the fabric of the book, with a warning to the reader that these symbols are not always limited in their interpretation to one particular equivalent. Novelists very seldom write their books as though they were mathematical equations, and Orwell was no exception.

In the course of *Nineteen Eighty-Four* Orwell makes many references to dust, usually with a view to adding to the sense of foreboding that is so characteristic of the book. Winston returns to Victory Mansions (Part One, Chapter 1, p.5) accompanied by 'a swirl of gritty dust', and, having begun his diary, is interrupted by his neighbour Mrs Parsons, who wants him to unblock her sink. Mrs Parsons lives in terror of her two children who are later to betray her husband to the Thought Police, and it is significant that when Winston looks at her he 'had the impression that there was dust in the creases of her face' (Part One, Chapter 2, p.20). Winston returns to his diary, and when it is time to leave for work, places 'an identifiable grain of whitish dust' (Part One, Chapter 2, p.26) on the cover of the book, the removal of which will tell him whether the diary has been discovered. Ironically, he learns later that even this precaution was known to the Thought Police.

Two instances of Orwell's use of the dust symbol are connected with Julia, and foreshadow the unhappy end to her affair with Winston. One evening while out walking, the pair are thrown off their feet by the blast from a rocket bomb. Winston fears that Julia is dead, but finds that her 'deathly white' face is covered with 'some powdery stuff' (Part Two, Chapter 3, p.106) which turns out to be plaster from a demolished building. On another occasion the lovers meet in the tower of a ruined church and make love. However, it is significant that their happiness takes place on 'the dusty, twig-littered floor' (Part Two, Chapter 3, p.106).

I have written in some detail in the Notes about Orwell's use of the symbol of the paperweight which Winston buys from Mr Charrington. Nevertheless, it may be useful to bring some of the references together at this point. When Winston buys it (Part One, Chapter 8, pp.78–80) he is attracted by its beauty and the fact that it seems to belong to a different age. However, when he leaves the junk-shop and spots Julia (whom he immediately believes to be spying on him) he walks away in the wrong direction while 'The lump of glass in his pocket banged against his thigh at each step, and he was half minded to take it out and throw it away' (Part One, Chapter 8, p.84). It could be said that the weight of the paperweight here represents the temptation to be rid of the idea of Julia, although, of course, they have not yet begun their love affair. Later in the novel the paperweight becomes an emblem of their own secret world (Part Two, Chapter 4, p.112 and p.120), while it is brutally smashed when the guards eventually break in on Winston and Julia (Part Two, Chapter 9, p.177).

Style

Much of the material dealt with in earlier sections such as 'Structure', 'Settings' and 'Symbolism' can be said to contribute towards a discussion of Orwell's style, as all of these go to make up his individual way of planning and writing the novel. However, in addition to points already raised, the student may find it helpful to have attention directed to certain recurrent verbal features of Orwell's writing in *Nineteen Eighty-Four*.

Many chapters of the book open with a very short simple sentence, plunging the reader into the middle of a situation or bringing him up to date with the action. Instances of this technique are: 'Winston was dreaming of his mother' (Part One, Chapter 3, p.26); 'Syme had vanished' (Part Two, Chapter 5, p.120); 'It had happened at last' (Part Two, Chapter 6, p.128); 'They had done it, they had done it at last!' (Part Two, Chapter 8, p.136).

Other devices employed frequently by Orwell in this novel are the use of lists and repetition of particular sentence structures. Examples of Orwell's piling up detail in list form are to be found in his description of the prole woman – '. . . her life had been laundering, scrubbing, darning, cooking, sweeping, polishing, mending, scrubbing, laundering . . .' (Part Two, Chapter 9, p.175), and the emphasis on verbs in Part Three,

Chapter 2, p.194 when the interrogators *slapped* his face, *wrung* his ears, *pulled* his hair, *made* him *stand* on one leg, *refused* him leave to *urinate, shone* glaring lights in his face (my italics).

Orwell often uses particular sentence structures when he wants to create a rhetorical effect. There are many examples in the novel, for instance in the repetition of sentences beginning 'It was he . . .' concerning O'Brien in Part Three, Chapter 2, pp.195–6, and the use of 'they' six times in six lines (five times beginning a new sentence) in Part Three, Chapter 4 p.220. In the same chapter (p.224) Winston's state of mind is reinforced by the sentence structure used: 'There were no more doubts, no more arguments, no more pain, no more fear.'

In general, the style of *Nineteen Eighty-Four* conforms to Orwell's ideal of good prose, which he said should be 'like a window-pane', but finally it should be noted that one or two instances of awkward repetition crept into the novel which Orwell would probably have eradicated if he had not been writing under the pressure of illness. He over-uses one particular metaphor to indicate fear: in Part One, Chapter 8, p.84 Winston's 'heart seemed to turn to ice and his bowels to water'; later 'Winston's entrails seemed to have turned into ice' (Part Two, Chapter 9, p.176), and, faced with the prospect of the rats in Room 101, 'His bowels seemed to turn to water' (Part Three, Chapter 5, p.228). In defence of Orwell it can be said that the metaphor is apt even if he uses it too often, and that there are very few other examples of clumsy writing in the book.

Characterization

Although *Nineteen Eighty-Four* contains a moderate number of named characters, if we count those who live in Victory Mansions and work at the Ministry of Truth, most readers will, I believe, finish the novel feeling that they know only three of them well – Winston, Julia and O'Brien. Indeed, some readers will feel that only Winston is fully drawn. A question is therefore raised concerning the quality of Orwell's power of characterization. Was he unable to draw rounded characters in any number in this novel, or did he deliberately choose to sketch in certain characters in outline, allowing his readers full knowledge only of the three who play a major part in the book?

The first point that needs to be made is that Orwell was trying to portray a world in which individuality was in the process of being stamped out. Winston is introduced as a rebel against the Party system, but a secret rebel. He wishes to establish his individuality by reacting against the Party, but he is not able to revolt openly. Later in the novel the reader learns, together with Winston, that Julia is another dissident, but she also has to hide her real feelings from the girls who live in her hostel and her fellow workers. Winston and Julia must be assumed to be two rebels among many who accept the faceless system. The Party exists to eradicate individuality. Therefore it is quite appropriate that Orwell should only portray Winston and a very few other characters as fully developed individuals.

Another point to be considered is that Orwell's narrative depends to a great extent on the fact that the story is told through the actions, reactions and memories of Winston Smith. We are made aware of scenes and events largely as Winston experiences them. We see inside his mind as he remembers dreams and events of his past life. Sometimes he is allowed by Orwell to share these memories with Julia and tell her about them, but more frequently we are there inside Winston's head experiencing events as he experiences them, sharing his view of situations, basing our assessment of possibilities on evidence provided by Winston alone. At times it is hard to realize that *Nineteen Eighty-Four* is not a novel narrated in the first person, so intimately do we get to know Winston.

Bearing these points in mind we see why Orwell chose to present minor characters in the novel by means of a few deft strokes only. Parsons, for instance, exists mainly in terms of physical details. The reader remembers him as a podgy individual who is always in the thick of things when community action is needed. He bears round with him the smell of stale sweat and it is appropriate that he should be the one to make the cell stink after using the lavatory in the Ministry of Love. Mrs Parsons is sketched in economically by Orwell. Her dusty face, reflecting the fear of her two monstrous children, is quite sufficient for his purpose. The reader does not wish or need to see deeply into her mind. Winston's philologist colleague, Syme, is another who is portrayed effectively yet without a great deal of individuality. In order to put across information about Newspeak without boring his readers, Orwell needed to add variety by introducing a character who could talk about the Newspeak Dictionary in a way that would be acceptable within a novel. Winston, as a rectifier of records in the Ministry of Truth, would naturally be interested in learning more about Syme's work, so that the information is transmitted to the reader as well as Winston by a character who is quite adequately drawn for Orwell's purpose. In addition Syme is given a hint of mystery in that Orwell makes Winston realize that he is too clever for his own good, so that it comes as no surprise when Syme later disappears (Part Two, Chapter 5, p.120).

Minor characters such as Ampleforth and Mr Charrington are effectively and economically presented. They play their part in the novel without ever attracting too much of the reader's interest as individuals. Other minor characters who are important in the book are not even sufficiently individualized by Orwell to merit the possession of names. In *Nineteen Eighty-Four* the proles play a large part symbolically, since Winston believes that if the Party is to be overthrown it must come via a proletarian rebellion. The old man whom Winston meets in the prole pub (Part One, Chapter 8) is important in so far as he is goodhearted but a disappointment to Winston, who wishes to probe his memories to discover the degree of distortion in the Party's version of the past. More important than the old man in the scheme of the novel, however, is the singing washerwoman who seems eternally to be hanging out babies' napkins in the yard below the room rented by Winston and Julia over Mr Charrington's shop. I have drawn attention in the textual notes (Part Two, Chapter 4 and Part Two, Chapter 9) to some of the important functions performed by this character, who acts as an ironic commentator (unbeknown to herself) on the lovers' situation. In connection with Orwell's emphasis on the character of the prole washerwoman, it is probably intentional that the only character shown by Orwell to have any spirit in the prison scenes in Part Three is the 'enormous wreck of a woman, aged about sixty, with great tumbling breasts and thick coils of white hair which had come down in her struggles', who tries to kick the guards who carry her into the cell, and yells curses after them as they go out.

Winston

Winston Smith, who works in the Records Department at the Ministry of Truth, is the central character in *Nineteen Eighty-Four*. He is present in every episode of the novel and it is through him that the story is told. We share his thoughts and memories, and are present with him throughout the action, following him from his first moments of rebellion to his emergence as a re-educated follower of Big Brother when he sits in the Chestnut Tree Café after his release from the Ministry of Love.

Several critics, among them John Atkins and Robert A. Lee, have made the point that Winston's name combines the most common English surname with the Christian name of Britain's remarkable leader during the Second World War, Winston Churchill. In this name, therefore, Orwell has linked Everyman with an exceptional man, preparing his readers for the courageous actions of rebellion against the Party to emerge from this (in some ways) very ordinary person. Elsewhere, I have made the point that Orwell's purpose demanded that his hero figure should not be a superman, in contrast to the leading character in Jack London's *The Iron Heel*. In fact, Winston's ordinariness is insisted on from the outset. He is verging on middle age, he has false teeth and a varicose ulcer. His wife has left him and on the rare occasions when he needs a sexual outlet he visits prostitutes. In spite of his burgeoning discontent with the Party which causes him to wish to overthrow it, he is by no means totally unlike other characters who approve of the regime, as we can see from his reactions to the war film described in Part One, Chapter 1, p.10.

Nevertheless, in spite of the fact that from the beginning Winston realizes that rebellion against the Party is doomed to failure, he has sufficient integrity and intellectual awareness of the ways in which people are manipulated in Oceania to search for means of revolt. He begins by starting a diary in an endeavour to pin down the truth. In a world in which everything is dominated by having to pretend to think what the Party wants him to think, he wishes to record how things really are. In this he is handicapped by the Party's control of the sources of information, so that he is not even absolutely sure of the year when he starts the diary.

At this point it is necessary to consider Winston's attitude towards his work at the Ministry in relation to his own difficulties in achieving a rebellion against the Party. For the purposes of the novel it was necessary for Orwell to give Winston the job he has in the book. Winston has to know how the Party manipulates the media so that he can know what he is rebelling against, and so that Orwell can transmit information about Newspeak and allied matters to his readers in a manner that is acceptable within a novel. Nevertheless, some readers have found an essential contradiction in Winston's character in that he wishes to fight against the Party, and yet we are told that 'Winston's greatest pleasure in life was in his work' (Part One, Chapter 4, p.38). In the course of Part One, Chapter 4, Winston is shown inventing a certain Comrade Ogilvy, and giving him a full and glorious past in order to provide faked material for rewriting one of Big Brother's speeches that has proved to be politically unacceptable and needs to be rectified for the records. Winston's task of rewriting is wittily described by Orwell, but we are perhaps justified in being disturbed by Winston's evident zest for the job.

In the early stages of the novel Winston is shown as relatively mild-mannered and ready to fit in with those with whom he comes into contact. He helps Mrs Parsons by unblocking her sink, talks with Syme and Parsons in the canteen, and is obviously an accepted member of the community both at work and at Victory Mansions. However, beneath the surface it is very different. He is full of violent passion against the Party, and this finds its outlet in the frenzied fantasies he has about Julia before he knows her (Part One, Chapter 1, p.16). When he is able to speak to her for the first time (Part Two, Chapter 1, p.87) it is significant that he picks her up when she falls in the corridor, even though he still believes her to be an enemy at that point.

It is this action of generosity that leads to his relationship with Julia. She slips him a note and from then on their relationship develops. Because of his love for Julia he gives up drinking Victory Gin, puts on weight, and his varicose ulcer, a symbol of his unhappiness and isolation, subsides, 'leaving only a brown stain on the skin above his ankle' (Part Two, Chapter 5, p.123). After beginning his affair with Julia, Winston is able to confess to his feelings of guilt about his mother and sister and recognize his earlier actions as intolerably selfish.

The love affair develops, but for Winston there has to be an intellectual element. In this he may be contrasted with Julia, for whom love and sex are sufficient. Winston wants Julia to be sexually corrupt, as this will prove that the Party is vulnerable. Some readers have found this reaction of Winston's unlikely, but there is no doubt that for him their love is 'a political act' (Part Two, Chapter 2, p.104).

When Winston and Julia go to O'Brien's flat, believing him to be a member of the Brotherhood, Winston is much more dominant than Julia although he naturally defers to O'Brien. When they next meet in the room over Mr Charrington's shop in the following chapter (Part Two, Chapter 9) Winston is the one who is anxious to read Goldstein's book, whereas Julia falls asleep while listening to him read aloud. However, when the guards invade the room Winston's intellect fails to protect him; he becomes rigid with fear, and does not even dare to look at Julia, who is writhing about on the floor after being hit in the solar plexus. At the conclusion of the chapter (pp.178–9), he realizes how he has been duped by Mr Charrington.

In Part Three of the novel Winston is drawn into close conjunction with O'Brien: torturer and tortured form two halves of one picture, and Winston even grows to love O'Brien, hideously though he is treated at the latter's command. The sections of the book which take place in the Ministry of Love show Winston forced to undergo humiliation upon humiliation before he is ready to let O'Brien believe that he is ready to conform. But Winston thinks that he can retain an inner integrity while conforming outwardly. O'Brien sees through his stratagem and breaks him completely by the threat of the rats in Room 101. At this point Winston is reduced to less than nothing, crying out for his punishment to be transferred to Julia. The rebel has capitulated totally. Readers' responses to Winston's breakdown will vary, but which of us can say what his own reaction would be to the intolerable?

Almost more horrifying than the episode in Room 101 is the aftermath. Winston had been beaten and tortured in the Ministry of Love, prior to being bathed, given new clothing and new dentures. Then came Room 101. After his display there he is released from the Ministry, and given a sinecure working in a desultory fashion on a committee at the Ministry of Truth. His days are spent in drinking and trying to forget the horrors of the Ministry of Love and the way in which he had reacted to them. The Chestnut Tree Café, haunt of traitors, is where he spends most of his time. In the final chapter he remembers a meeting with Julia after they had both been released, during which it was evident that they had each lost all feeling for the other. Winston also recalls one of the few relatively happy occasions spent with his mother and the small sister to whom he had behaved so badly at other times, but rejects the memory, as it does not fit in with the Party orthodoxy he is now striving to attain. While sitting in the café he has been calculating the chances of a victory for Oceania in the war. When the news is broadcast that Oceania is victorious, Winston's life comes full circle as he gazes adoringly at the poster of Big Brother on the wall, and realizes that he now loves him without question.

Julia

Julia has been described by Harold Nicolson as a lay figure in the novel, and it is true that she is not explored in any great depth; but Orwell makes good use of her both as an extension of and as a contrast to Winston Smith. He shows great skill in the way in which she is made to play a significant part in Winston's thoughts before he even speaks to her. In Part One she is referred to on a number of occasions and it is evident that she attracts Winston even though he suspects that she is a loyal follower of the Party. In Part One, Chapter 1, pp.11–12, Julia is introduced for the first time. We learn that she works in the Ministry of Truth and has a 'mechanical job on one of the novel-writing machines'. Immediately a contrast is made between her practical skill and Winston's work involving the mind. Julia is an attractive young woman 'of about twenty-seven, with thick dark hair, a freckled face, and swift, athletic movements'. Her Junior Anti-Sex League sash contrasts with her femininity and misleads Winston into believing that she is a bigoted adherent of the Party. Nevertheless he is physically attracted to her and has sexual fantasies about her.

In Part One of the book Julia is unnamed, and is usually referred to as 'the dark-haired girl'. Winston receives a terrible fright when he almost bumps into her on leaving Mr Charrington's shop (Part One, Chapter 8, p.84), and he even contemplates following her and killing her with a cobblestone or the paperweight which he has just bought. At the beginning of Part Two Julia slips Winston her note and thus begins their love affair. She shows great resourcefulness in telling him where to see her after work when he is able to sit near her in the canteen (Part Two, Chapter 1, p.93), and also when she arranges for them to meet in the countryside. When they do meet in the country Julia takes the lead and tells Winston that she is probably better at finding things out than he is (Part Two, Chapter 2, p.99), but she is gentle with him, particularly when he proves impotent when they first try to make love. She reveals to Winston that she hates the Party and sees through the hypocrisy of many of its members. Her rebellion, however, is confined to thinking, to buying goods on the black market and to making love with Party members, but not with members of the Inner Party whom she despises. In response to Winston's questioning she reveals that she has had many lovers and that she takes delight in the sexual act for its own sake, apart from being attracted to Winston himself.

As the novel proceeds we learn more about Julia and through her gain more information about the workings of the Ministry of Truth. Her animal vigour and a kind of innate optimism contrast with Winston's conviction that their rebellion is bound to end in death. As Orwell states, 'With Julia, everything came back to her own sexuality', and he causes

Winston to think that 'she still expected something from life' (Part Two, Chapter 3, p.109 and p.111). Her practicality is again stressed when she brings black-market goods to the room they take over the junk-shop, and by her promise to block up the rat-hole in the wainscoting. When she makes herself up for Winston we also see how great Julia's deprivation has been in not being allowed by the Party to wear dresses and cosmetics (Part Two, Chapter 4, pp.116–17).

In addition to her role as Winston's mistress, Julia is important to the political aspects of *Nineteen Eighty-Four*. She has a greater capacity for original ideas than Winston and at one time startles him by suggesting that 'the rocket bombs which fell daily on London were probably fired by the Government of Oceania itself "just to keep people frightened" ' (Part Two, Chapter 5, p.125). Nevertheless, she is not interested in politics and is delighted to be characterized by Winston as 'only a rebel from the waist downwards' (Part Two, Chapter 5, p.127). When she and Winston go to O'Brien's flat in an attempt to join the Brotherhood, Julia plays a very subsidiary part in the proceedings. It is worth noting that she is the one to break in, before Winston does, to say that they are not prepared 'to separate and never see one another again.' (Part Two, Chapter 8, p.141), but otherwise she says little and is the first to leave.

Julia has earlier stated realistically that if caught they will obviously be forced to confess, but she does not think that the Party can make them believe anything they are forced to say under torture (Part Two, Chapter 7, p.136). Her commitment is to Winston, not to a remote political ideal, and it comes as no surprise when she falls asleep while he is reading aloud from Goldstein's book. She wakes with Winston and together they look out into the yard below at the prole woman pegging out napkins. The last we see of Julia until the final chapter of the book is when she is carried out of the room by the guards, having been felled by a fist 'doubling her up like a pocket ruler'

(Part Two, Chapter 9, p.177).

The final glimpse of Julia is as she is remembered by Winston after their release from prison. She tries to avoid him when he meets her in the Park, and he sees that she bears the marks of torture. She dislikes him now and tells him baldly that she betrayed him, saying that all you care about is yourself when threatened with something intolerable. Finally she walks away from Winston, her love for him eternally destroyed. Significantly, we are told that 'He followed irresolutely for a little distance, half a pace behind her' (Part Three, Chapter 6, p.235). Ironically, in their final meeting Julia still takes the lead, as she had done when instigating the love affair with Winston.

O'Brien

O'Brien exists in *Nineteen Eighty-Four* less as a fully drawn character than as a set of external characteristics. From the beginning he plays a large part in Winston's consciousness, and he is linked most strongly with him in the final stages of the novel, during the interrogation sequences in the Ministry of Love. Some have seen in O'Brien a parallel to Dostoevsky's Grand Inquisitor in *The Brothers Karamazov*, and there are undoubtedly similarities in the two characters and their functions. However, in the twentieth century it has become relatively commonplace for authors to present relationships between hunters and hunted, torturers and tortured, in a way that stresses the building up of a feeling almost of love between them. We can see this in certain kinds of detective story as well as in novels by writers such as Graham Greene. The portrayal of O'Brien depends to a considerable extent on the establishment of the connection with Winston.

We first hear of O'Brien when Winston recalls the Two Minutes Hate in the first chapter of *Nineteen Eighty-Four*. O'Brien is present in the Records Department when the Hate is due to begin, and he stays. As a member of the Inner Party he wears black overalls, and he is 'a large, burly man with a thick neck and a coarse, humorous, brutal face. In spite of his formidable appearance he had a certain charm of manner' (Part One, Chapter 1, p.12). Orwell makes a great deal of O'Brien's habit of resettling his spectacles on his nose, and of his general urbanity. Winston believes (for no clearly defined reason) that O'Brien is politically suspect. At the end of the Hate Winston believes that he catches a look of complicity from O'Brien (Part One, Chapter 1, p.17).

When Winston returns to his own flat after unblocking Mrs Parsons's sink he recalls a dream in which someone had said to him, 'We shall meet in the place where there is no darkness', and he is sure that it was O'Brien who spoke those words. Later in the novel Winston realizes that he is writing his diary for O'Brien (Part One, Chapter 7, p.68) – as ironically turns out to be the case.

Little further is heard of O'Brien until Part Two, Chapter 6, when he approaches Winston in a corridor and offers to lend him a copy of the new edition of the Newspeak Dictionary. Winston is struck by his 'disarming friendliness' and is convinced that he also is a rebel against the Party. Shortly afterwards Winston and Julia visit O'Brien's flat and are completely dominated by him. O'Brien takes total control and leads Winston and Julia on. He catechizes them about their willingness to commit any atrocities as members of a secret organization, and it is worth noting that his behaviour is reminiscent of that of a priest in several ways in this chapter.

Eventually, Winston comes face to face with O'Brien in the Ministry of Love, where the latter battles for his allegiance in a way that recalls a priest battling for a lost soul. In this section of the novel O'Brien, who reveals that he was partly responsible for writing Goldstein's book, has little to do but appear impressive to Winston and let him into the Party's secret for wanting to obtain power. He is revealed as an archetype of the modern totalitarian inquisitor who acts on behalf of a society that cannot afford to have martyrs. Winston must be broken and then put on show, just as many political prisoners have been in the last thirty years. O'Brien is dominant in these last scenes of *Nineteen Eighty-Four*, but Orwell does little to make him credible as an individual. He is a type – the bigot totally obsessed by his own creed, unable to allow the possibility of his being wrong. O'Brien is the finally perfected instrument of totalitarian power.

Bibliography

The student is advised to read as much of Orwell's work as possible, in particular *Homage to Catalonia* and *Animal Farm*, both of which are easily available in Penguin editions. Penguin also publish in four volumes *The Collected Essays, Journalism and Letters of George Orwell*, edited by Sonia Orwell and Ian Angus. Volume IV (*In Front of Your Nose*) deals with the period during which Orwell was writing *Nineteen Eighty-Four*.

There are now many books of criticism on Orwell, in addition to articles in journals. Some of these are referred to in this book, and are to be recommended to the advanced student. However, I have confined the following list to four books which are critically sound and readily available in cheap paperback editions:

B. T. Oxley *George Orwell*, in the 'Literature in Perspective' series (Evans Brothers)

Edward M. Thomas *Orwell*, in the 'Writers and Critics' series (Oliver and Boyd)

Raymond Williams *Orwell*, in 'Fontana Modern Masters' (Fontana/Collins)

George Woodcock *The Crystal Spirit: A Study of George Orwell* (Penguin)

Summaries of chapters, textual notes and revision questions

Part One

Chapter 1

Winston Smith, a 39-year-old worker in the Records Department of the Ministry of Truth, returns to his seventh-floor flat in Victory Mansions at lunchtime one day in April. The block of flats smells and the lift is not working, as the electricity has been cut off. Posters of the Party Leader, Big Brother, are in evidence everywhere, and a police helicopter patrol can be seen from the window. Inside the flat a two-way telescreen pumps out propaganda while each movement Winston makes can be observed.

The date is approximately 1984 and London is now the chief city of Airstrip One, the third most populous province of Oceania. The city bears the marks of bombing and decay, but is dominated by the towering buildings of four government Ministries, the Ministry of Truth, the Ministry of Peace, the Ministry of Love and the Ministry of Plenty.

Winston goes to an alcove out of range of the telescreen and makes the first entry in a secret diary he has decided to keep. He wishes to commit to paper his discontent with life under the Party regime, but finds it hard to begin writing. His first diary entry concerns a violent war film he had seen the previous evening, which had drawn applause from members of the Party but had been the cause of a noisy protest from a working-class woman who was affronted by the atrocities shown.

Winston then recalls an incident that had happened at work that morning. At eleven o'clock he had been present at the regular Two Minutes Hate, a show of organized mass hysteria directed principally against Emmanuel Goldstein, renegade who had once been a leading Party figure. Two persons present at the Two Minutes Hate made a particular impression on Winston: a dark-haired young woman who worked in the Fiction Department, and O'Brien, a member of the Inner Party. He distrusted the young woman while at the same time finding her sexually attractive. He had long felt drawn to O'Brien in the unsubstantiated belief that he was not totally committed to the Party. The Two Minutes Hate is described, during which Winston felt himself being carried away by the hysteria and directing his emotions against Goldstein, Big Brother and the young woman almost indiscriminately. At the end of the film which acted as a focus for the Two Minutes Hate, Winston caught O'Brien's eye and thought that he had detected a political sympathy there. He returned to his work wondering whether he had imagined it.

Coming out of his reverie Winston finds that he has unconsciously written DOWN WITH BIG BROTHER over half a page of his diary. He is aware of the inevitability of capture by the Thought Police in the long run, but is still startled when he hears a knocking at the door of his flat, thinking that his rebellion has already been detected.

the clocks . . . . . thirteen This is the first indication (apart from the title) that the novel is set in the future when a twenty-four-hour clock is the norm, but the reference to 'thirteen' also prefigures the ill fortune that is to be associated with Winston in the book.

nuzzled-Pressed.

Victory Mansions Note the irony of the name of the block of flats in which Winston lives. The inhabitants of this police state are, in a real sense, defeated. Winston also drinks Victory Gin (Part One, Chapter 1, p.8), smokes Victory cigarettes (Part One, Chapter 1, p.8) and arranges to meet Julia in Victory Square (Part Two, Chapter 1, p.93), which is the renamed Trafalgar Square.

more than a metre wide Another indication that the novel is set in the future; Britain has ceased to exist as a separate country using the yard as a unit of measurement.

the face . . . handsome features While *Nineteen Eighty-Four* was written as a warning against all forms of totalitarianism, this description particularly calls to mind posters of the Russian leader, Joseph Stalin (1879–1953), which were displayed during the Second World War in Britain. Russia and Britain were then allies.

varicose ulcer An ulcer caused by permanent dilatation of the veins. Orwell stresses this feature to emphasize that Winston is no superman.

pig-iron Iron in pigs, which are oblong masses of metal from smelting furnaces.

the Party This is the first indication that Winston is living in a one-party state.

coarse soap . . . blades The irritating shortage of basic commidities emphasized in the novel (see, for example, Part One, Chapter 1, p.9, and Part One, Chapter 2, p.24) reflects the state of affairs in Britain during and immediately following the Second World War.

INGSOC The first reference in the novel to Newspeak, the official language of Oceania. Ingsoc means 'English Socialism' (see Part One, Chapter 3, p.32), but it should be noted that Orwell stated that *Nineteen Eighty-Four* was not intended as an attack on Socialism nor on the British Labour Party.

Three-Year Plan Compare the situation in Russia under Stalin, when a series of Five-Year Plans took place, aimed primarily at industrial expansion. Production targets were set for various industries. The first Five-Year Plan began in 1928.

the Ministry . . . landscape The descriptions of the Ministry of Truth are based largely upon Orwell's experiences of the BBC and the Ministry of Information during the Second World War. The Ministry of Information was located in London University's Senate House, which towers above Bloomsbury.

willow-herb A common plant with pale purple flowers, frequently seen on bombed sites in Britain at the time when Orwell was writing the novel.

ramifications Subdivisions.

The Ministry of Love . . . frightening one This reference, followed almost immediately by the fact that Winston had never been inside the Ministry of Love, is ironic in view of the end of the novel, when he is tortured inside the building.

guards in black uniforms In choosing black for the colour of the guards' uniforms and for the overalls of Inner Party members (see Part One, Chapter 1, p.12) Orwell probably had in mind the uniforms of Hitler's secret state police, the Gestapo.

He had seen . . . possess it Winston's urge to own the book, which he guessed to be very old, is indicative of his wish to preserve the past. His work at the Ministry of Truth consists of distorting the past by altering printed records. He aims to counteract this by keeping a diary.

nothing was illegal . . . any laws One of the most chilling statements in the novel. The Party is able to command absolute obedience without recourse to the law.

speak-write Newspeak for a dictating machine which records what is spoken in the form of print.

To begin with . . . 1984 Winston's writing of the date serves two purposes: it informs us how far in the future the events take place, and his uncertainty regarding the exact year shows the Party's total control of information.

One very good one . . . Mediterranean Winston's reactions to the horrors of the war film show that in some ways he is very little different from others who are staunch Party supporters. Notice how he moves from an objective stance, referring to the 'audience', to describing things in a way that reflects his own involvement in the film. Observe the repetition of 'you saw'.

jewess Orwell probably had in mind the persecution of the Jews by the Nazi party in the 1930s and during the Second World War.

prole Proletarian. The prole woman's outburst prepares us for Winston's diary entry which opens Part One, Chapter 7, p.59, and for the emphasis on the singing woman pegging out washing (Part Two, Chapter 4, pp.113 and 116, and Part Two, Chapter 9, pp.173–5).

One of them was a girl . . . of her hips Significantly, Orwell has Winston recall Julia before passing on to O'Brien. His relationship with her is to be the cause of his falling into the latter's power. Note the irony of the Junior Anti-Sex League sash emphasizing Julia's femininity.

It was because of the atmosphere . . . carry about with her Winston's dislike of Julia (which conceals attraction) centres on what he believes to be her commitment to Party ideology. In Part Two, Chapter 2, p.103, he discovers how wrong his earlier impressions have been.

But at any rate . . . get him alone Ironic in view of Winston's interrogation by O'Brien in Part Three.

Goldstein Orwell had the Russian revolutionary Leon Trotsky (1879–1940) in mind when he conceived Goldstein. Note the Jewish name (Trotsky was originally called Bronstein), the emphasis on the beard and spectacles, and the direct reference to the title of Trotsky's *The Revolution Betrayed* (1937) in Goldstein's speech (p.14).

renegade Deserter of a party, turncoat. Goldstein's position in the novel can be compared with that of Snowball in *Animal Farm*. Both are useful scapegoats.

deviations Departures from the Party line. In Russia those who departed from Communist doctrines were abused as deviationists.

diaphragm The large muscular partition separating the thorax from the abdomen.

aureole Halo.

goatee beard A small beard on the point of the chin.

compendium Summary.

clandestinely Secretly.

heretic Holder of an unorthodox opinion.

the doubt that . . . very existence Another example of the Party's total control of information.

Vivid, beautiful hallucinations . . . climax Winston's dislike of Julia causes him to have violent sexual fantasies about her.

Saint Sebastian A legendary martyr whose feast day is commemorated on 20 January. Almost nothing is known of him, but traditionally he is supposed to have been an officer of the Roman imperial guard in Diocletian's time. When it was revealed that he was a Christian he was sentenced to be shot with arrows. His wounds were healed by the widow of another martyr, but Diocletian then had him beaten to death with cudgels.

climax Orgasm.

But . . . the face of Big Brother . . . wear off immediately Orwell seems to have had in mind the possibility of producing films containing subliminal images which communicate their messages below the level at which the conscious mind can perceive them. In the 1950s American advertisers experimented with subliminal techniques to promote their products.

deep, slow, rhythmical chant . . . Brings to mind the chanting of 'Sieg Heil' by Hitler's followers at Nazi rallies in the 1930s.

Such incidents . . . sequel Ironic, in view of later events.

equivocal Ambiguous, capable of a twofold interpretation.

You might dodge . . . bound to get you Even at this early stage in his rebellion Winston is aware of the inevitable outcome.

It was always at night . . . during the night The description of the arrests reflects the practice of, for example, the Gestapo.

Chapter 2

Winston opens the door to discover a neighbour, Mrs Parsons, the wife of one of his fellow employees. She wants him to unblock her sink, as her husband is out. He does so and is about to return to his own flat when the two Parsons children, who belong to the Spies, the Party's juvenile organization, involve him against his will in a game in which they pretend he is a traitor to the Party. Winston is shot by a catapult on the back of the neck by the Parsons boy. When he returns to his own flat he reflects that the Party has captured the imagination of the young by means of organizations such as the Spies, and that parents are now constantly afraid of being denounced by their children.

Winston remembers a dream he had some seven years previously in which O'Brien seemed to speak to him. He considers the weight of the Party forces against any possibility of effective rebellion, and recognizes that his diary will only ever be read by the Thought Police. Nevertheless, he once more starts to write in his diary in the few minutes before he has to return to work. He washes tell-tale traces of ink from his fingers, and places a grain of whitish dust on the cover of his diary so that he will know if the book is moved by the Thought Police in his absence.

comrade A form of address used principally in Soviet Russia to denote equality.

discountenanced Discouraged.

Youth League and the Spies Organizations by means of which the Party attracted support among the young. The description of their activities later in the chapter (p.23) is reminiscent of the Hitler Youth movement in Nazi Germany.

organizing community hikes . . . demonstrations Note the contradiction in terms of 'organizing' and 'spontaneous'.

invertebrate Used figuratively here to mean irresolute, hesitant.

Winston raised his hands . . . a game The boy's viciousness, together with the reference later in the chapter to a 'child hero' denouncing its parents to the Thought Police (p.23), prepares us for the denunciation of Parsons by his little daughter (see Part Three, Chapter 1, p.187).

salt mines Forced labour in the salt mines of Siberia was a common punishment for deviationists in Soviet Russia.

There was a link . . . come true Notice the emphasis on the connection between Winston and O'Brien. In Part Three they do 'meet in the place where there is no darkness' – the Ministry of Love (Part Three, Chapter 1, p.184).

Bad news . . . grammes to twenty One of many indications in the novel of how the Party manipulates news to its own advantage. Because of his job Winston is well aware of the techniques used.

Somewhere far away . . . at present Orwell is here making use of his memories of flying bombs and rockets which endangered London and South-East England during 1944 and the early months of 1945.

mutability Liability to change.

He was alone . . . his side The prominence given here to Winston's isolation reminds us that Orwell considered *The Last Man in Europe* as a title for the novel.

Nothing was . . . your skull Ironic in view of the events of Part Three.

To the future . . . greetings! A very moving moment in the novel. Winston reaches out from his loneliness and tries to communicate with a better age, while recognizing that it is certain that he will be caught and his diary will be destroyed by the Thought Police.

zealot Fanatical partisan.

With the tip . . . was moved We learn later that the Thought Police carefully replaced the speck of whitish dust on the cover of the diary (Part Three, Chapter 4, p.222).

Chapter 3

The chapter begins with Winston dreaming of his mother, who had disappeared nearly thirty years before. In his dream he sees his mother and sister in a sinking ship, looking up at him through the darkening water. He is aware that he is somehow responsible for their deaths. Winston's dream changes and he believes himself to be in an idyllic country setting. The dark-haired girl from the Fiction Department comes towards him and strips herself with a graceful gesture.

Winston is then awakened by a whistle from the telescreen, and is forced to take part in physical exercises. While doing so he reflects on the ways in which the Party has gained total control of factual information. His day-dreaming is sharply interrupted by the voice of the instructress from the telescreen, who praises his next attempt at touching his toes.

purges Movements to get rid of people regarded as undesirable. There were several notorious purges in Russia in the 1930s.

He could not remember . . . sacrificed to his own Winston's guilt feelings about his mother and sister are referred to elsewhere in the novel. (e.g. Part Two, Chapter 7, pp.131–4, and Part Three, Chapter 6, pp.237–8).

the Golden Country Note the contrast with the descriptions of urban scenes in the novel. Winston's dream of freedom seeks its outlet in the world of nature, but also includes 'leaves . . . like women's hair', which leads on immediately to the description of the 'girl with dark hair'.

dace Small fresh-water fish.

With what seemed . . . white and smooth See Part Two, Chapter 2, pp.102–03.

Clothing coupons Another parallel with the situation in Britain during the Second World War. The Board of Trade introduced clothes rationing, and individuals were issued with booklets of detachable tickets or coupons which had to be surrendered when purchases of clothing were made.

Physical Jerks Organized exercises.

Yapped. . . . female voice Orwell economically portrays the instructress by the use of words like 'yapped', 'rapped', 'barked', 'screamed' and 'shrewish'.

When there were no . . . lost its sharpness The Party's control of men's minds is reinforced here, and by the use of 'he felt fairly certain', 'could not definitely remember', and 'Perhaps it was the time . . .'.

Tube station At the height of the Blitz in the Second World War many London underground railway stations were used as air-raid shelters by large numbers of people. Once again Orwell is relating conditions in 1984 to those that he himself knew.

gyrating Revolving.

Only in his own . . . be annihilated Presumably Winston is thinking of a time when he will be dead, but in Part Three we see that O'Brien does not intend to wait until then to annihilate his consciousness.

labyrinthine Complicated, almost impenetrable.

In the Party histories ... glass sides Compare the way in which the *History of the All-Union Communist Party (Bolsheviks)*, published in 1938, selected 1912 for the official establishment of the party rather than an earlier date, thereby making it possible to give Stalin greater prominence than was due to him.

capitalists People who had accumulated wealth which was then invested to produce more wealth.

Smith! . . . 6079 Smith W.! A dramatic interruption of Winston's dangerous thoughts. Note how the number and the surname followed by the initial further depersonalize Winston, a system much used by armies to eradicate individuality.

We don't all . . . in the front line Not intended ironically by the instructress.

Chapter 4

Winston is at his desk at the Ministry of Truth beginning his day's work of rectifying articles and news-items for the file copies of newspapers kept by the Party. This is necessary to maintain the Party's reputation for infallibility. The immense complexity of the Records Department is described, together with the functions of the Ministry as a whole. After an interruption for the Two Minutes Hate Winston continues with his work, in the course of which he invents a non-existent Comrade Ogilvy whose 'life history' will be printed in *The Times* in place of a speech by Big Brother which has proved to be counter to present Party policy.

pneumatic tube A tube along which papers, packages, etc, are conveyed by means of compressed air.

orifices Apertures, openings.

memory holes. Ironic, since the holes exist to obliterate written records.

With a faint feeling of satisfaction Here, and later in the chapter (p.38), Orwell emphasizes that Winston's greatest pleasure lies in his work. By demonstrating Winston's skill he is able to transmit a great deal of information about the workings of the Ministry of Truth in a way that holds the reader's interest.

collated Compared in detail with the material in the original copy.

ideological Connected with the ideas forming the basis of an economic or political system.

palimpsest Manuscript from which the original writing has been removed to make room for a second piece.

political alignment Alliances between Oceania, Eurasia and Eastasia.

definitive texts Texts to be regarded as final, not subject to revision.

And this hall . . . multitude of jobs Note Orwell's use of terms connected with bees in this section – 'workers', 'cell', 'swarms'. The effect is to show the relative unimportance of individuals, and the intense activity in the Records Department.

repositories Places where things are deposited for safety or preservation.

treatise A written composition dealing thoroughly with the principles of a subject.

There was a whole . . . versificator Orwell is here stating, in an exaggerated way, the situation that has existed in Britain since the production of the first cheap newspapers and magazines towards the end of the nineteenth century.

Order of Conspicuous Merit, Second Class Compare the situation in Communist Russia, where such decorations are awarded in a society ostensibly devoted to promoting a classless structure. In *Animal Farm* the military decorations, 'Animal Hero, First Class' and 'Animal Hero, Second Class', were created after the Battle of the Cowshed (Penguin edition, p.40).

The great purges . . . couple of years See note on 'purges' in Part One, Chapter 3.

Winston wondered . . . had actually said Orwell may have had in mind the situation existing in the big Hollywood film studios in the 1930s, when it was common practice for several writers to be working separately on a script, each under the impression that he was the only one.

Sometimes they were released . . . executed Compare the situation of Jones, Aaronson and Rutherford (Part One, Chapter 7, p.64).

ghostly Used here metaphorically.

At the age of three . . . traitors generally This invented description can be paralleled by reference to actual speeches and newspaper reports from Russia and Communist China today.

total abstainer A person who drinks no alcohol.

celibacy Abstinence from marriage.

Once again . . . opposite cubicle Note how Orwell adds variety to what is basically a very static chapter by means of references to Tillotson. Here, and on pages 36, 37 and 39, he makes Winston very aware of Tillotson, thus adding a kind of drama to what is basically expository writing.

Chapter 5

At lunchtime in the Ministry canteen Winston meets Syme, a philologist friend, and they are joined by Parsons after Syme has explained some of the principles of Newspeak to Winston. At the next table Winston is aware of a young woman and a man of about thirty whose strident voice causes him to feel horror at the mindless quality it conveys. Winston reflects that one day Syme will be vaporized because he is too intelligent. Parsons collects a subscription for Hate Week from Winston and describes the activities of his little daughter in the Spies.

An announcement from the Ministry of Plenty is broadcast which causes Winston to consider the way in which everyone but himself appears to be taken in by Party propaganda. Winston becomes aware of being looked at by the girl at the next table, who turns out to be the dark-haired girl who sat near him during the Two Minutes Hate attended by O'Brien. He fears that she may be a member of the Thought Police or an enthusiastic amateur spy.

philologist An expert in the science of language.

It was a good hanging, . . . tablet The unsavoury quality of Syme's remarks is very appropriate in view of the emphasis on the squalid atmosphere of the canteen.

a filthy liquid mess . . . meat Orwell is here insisting upon ugliness of detail to reinforce the point that the quality of life has declined in 1984. Note the use of terms indicating the difficulty of being sure what is being eaten, e.g. 'pinkish stuff', 'probably a preparation of meat'. A similar point is made by Orwell in *Coming up for Air* (1939) when his hero, George Bowling, bites into a frankfurter which contains fish (Penguin edition pp.26–7).

synonyms Words having the same meaning as others of the same language.

antonyms Words having the opposite meaning to others of the same language.

In your heart . . . shades of meaning Note how Orwell allows Syme to have this insight into Winston's real feelings, even while his main reason for including the character is to give readers information about Newspeak.

Except the proles See note on 'prole' in Part One, Chapter 1.

One of these days . . . will disappear See Part Two, Chapter 5, pp.120–21.

Winston had a curious . . . dummy The strident man represents everything that Winston is striving not to be.

yet the place was somehow ill-omened A sinister reference which points forward to Winston's situation in the last chapter of the book.

I tell you . . . flags in the whole street Orwell appears to have had in mind the decorating of streets and blocks of flats that happened in Britain to celebrate victory in Europe and victory over Japan in May and August 1945, VE and VJ day respectively.

two creased and filthy notes Another reference meant to emphasize squalor.

there is a war on A saying frequently heard in Britain during the Second World War, usually used by shopkeepers and others to justify shortages or unpleasant conditions.

How easy it was . . . even predominated The reference to the Party's ideal physical type calls to mind Hitler's emphasis on the same qualities in Nazi Germany.

Parsons, stirred to vague . . . you can let me have? An excellent example of the effectiveness of Party propaganda. Note the contrast between the two sentences spoken by Parsons, and the fact that he cannot see the contradiction that is implied.

Parsons . . . never be vaporized However, see Part Three, Chapter 1, p.187, in which Winston meets Parsons in the Ministry of Love.

The girl at the next . . . intensity The girl with dark hair has been the last person in Winston's thoughts. It is very effective to have him now notice her in reality.

but then it was precisely . . . danger of all Compare the reference to Parsons' little daughter earlier in the chapter (p.49).

tic A twitch of the facial muscles.

B.B. Big Brother.

Chapter 6

The chapter begins with Winston making an entry in his diary about an encounter with a seemingly young prostitute three years before. He finds the recollection painful and has to force himself to continue writing. The memory of the prostitute causes him to think about the Party's attitude to sex and marriage, and he remembers his unsatisfactory sex life with his wife, Katharine, from whom he has been separated for nearly eleven years. Winston continues writing about his meeting with the prostitute, and thinks resentfully that he will never be able to have a love affair with a woman of the Party because of their conditioning against sexual enjoyment. Returning to his diary, he remembers that when he saw the prostitute in the lamplight she was old and toothless, but, in spite of this, he had sexual intercourse with her. Winston finds that writing down a description of what happened fails to free him from its horror.

She was standing . . . bright red lips It is significant that Winston's account of his encounter with the prostitute follows on almost immediately after the description in Chapter 5 of the dark-haired girl who simultaneously attracts and frightens him. Another link is provided by the contrast between appearance and reality in both women. The prostitute "had a young face" (p.54), yet 'was quite an old woman' (p.58), while the girl seems to be an orthodox Party member, but turns out to be a rebel against its rules.

Your worst enemy . . . nervous system A point returned to elsewhere in the novel (e.g. Part One, Chapter 7, p.85: 'It struck him that in moments of crisis one is never fighting against an external enemy, but always against one's own body.') Significant in view of the ending.

fornication Sexual intercourse between an unmarried man and an unmarried woman. Note how the reference foreshadows the lovemaking between Winston and Julia in Part Two, Chapter 4, p.117.

The unforgivable crime . . . actually happening Yet Winston's rebellion is to be manifested largely through his affair with Julia.

eroticism Pleasure taken in sex.

enema An injection (usually of liquid) into the rectum.

artificial insemination A means of planting male seed within the womb of the female without sexual intercourse taking place.

aquiline With a hooked or curved nose.

whenever it was not impossible i.e. when she was not menstruating.

Katharine's white body . . . the Party Note the contrast with Julia's body, which 'gleamed white in the sun' (Part Two, Chapter 2, p.103).

scuffles Struggles, disorderly fights. The use of the word intentionally degrades the act of sexual intercourse.

The sexual act . . . rebellion A point returned to in Part Two, Chapter 2, p.103.

therapy Treatment of a disease with a view to curing it and preventing its recurrence. The word is used here as Winston hopes that by recording the episode with the old prostitute it will cease to bother him.

Chapter 7

Winston makes another entry in his diary, setting down his belief that if there is hope it lies in the proles. He thinks that only they have the power to overthrow the Party, but he realizes that they are not politically conscious. Winston has borrowed a children's history book from Mrs Parsons and copies a passage from it into his diary. He reflects on the impossibility of discovering the truth about the past now that all records are under Party control, but he feels instinctively that life in 1984 is worse than it was before the Revolution. Winston remembers the only time when he could have proved that the Party falsified evidence. A photograph came into his possession of three surviving leaders of the Revolution who had been discredited by the Party, and this showed that they could not have been traitors to the Party as they had later confessed to being. Winston had destroyed the photograph.

Winston contemplates the horrifying possibility that one day the Party will announce that two and two make five and everybody will have to believe it, but, recalling O'Brien, for whom he feels he is keeping his diary, he resolves to hold on to self-evident facts, as they constitute the basis of freedom.

They needed only to rise . . . shaking off flies This reminds us that in *Animal Farm* the workers are represented by Boxer, the carthorse, but that he is totally submissive to Napoleon, the dictator figure.

indoctrinate Teach, instruct.

The great majority . . . in their homes This reinforces the lack of importance attached to the proles by the Party, and also prepares us for the fact that Mr Charrington says that he does not have a telescreen (Part One, Chapter 8, p.81).

lawn A kind of fine linen.

The only evidence . . . must have been different Here Winston returns to the thoughts he had earlier in the canteen (Part One, Chapter 5, p.51).

Everything faded . . . act of falsification Orwell cleverly introduces variety here by leading into one of Winston's actual memories.

counter-revolutionaries Supporters of a revolution aimed at overthrowing the results of an earlier one.

Goldstein had fled . . . their crimes This parallels the situation in Russia in the 1930s when, as Elizabeth Wiskemann has written, 'Nearly all the recent leaders of the Soviet world were . . . indicted and slaughtered' (*Europe of the Dictators 1919–1945*).

intelligence Used here to mean 'betrayal of secret information'.

embezzlement Taking money fraudulently for one's own use.

sinecures Profitable jobs with no duties attached.

He had the feeling . . . Big Brother See note on the Party histories in Part One, Chapter 3.

They were corpses . . . the grave Effective metaphor which prepares us for Winston's statement, 'We are the dead' (Part Two, Chapter 3, p.111).

rehashing Putting old material into a new form without really changing it or improving it.

Under the spreading . . . chestnut tree This verse is based on a song composed about 1854 by W. H. Weiss, a setting of 'The Village Blacksmith', by H. W. Longfellow (1807–82). See also Part Three, Chapter 6, p.236.

both Aaronson . . . broken noses Presumably because of their treatment in prison.

a warning to posterity A Party-controlled warning, very unlike that Winston tries to record in his diary.

stratum Layer of deposited substance.

frontispiece Illustration facing the title-page of a book.

In the end the Party . . . believe it Important in view of later events in the novel (e.g. Part Three, Chapter 2, pp.200–207 and Part Three, Chapter 6, p.233). Significantly, Orwell had written in a book review in January 1939, 'It is quite possible that we are descending into an age in which two and two will make five when the Leader says so' (*The Collected Essays, Journalism and Letters of George Orwell*, Volume 1, item 147).

arrayed Marshalled, set out.

axiom Self-evident truth.

Chapter 8

One evening after leaving work Winston is wandering in a prole quarter of London. A rocket bomb explodes near him, but he is unharmed. He realizes that he is near the shop where he bought the book which he uses for his diary. He sees an old man enter a pub and follows him, hoping to question him about life before the Revolution. Winston's appearance in the prole pub attracts attention, but soon he is ignored. He gets into conversation with the old man, but is unable to obtain coherent information from him. A short while after leaving the pub Winston finds himself outside the junk-shop where he bought the diary. He goes in and buys a <u>glass paperweight</u> from the proprietor, <u>Mr Charrington</u>, who shows him another room upstairs. Winston thinks fleetingly of renting the room, but puts the idea out of his mind. On leaving the shop he sees the dark-haired girl from the Fiction Department coming towards him. He is sure that she is keeping an eye on him, and returns to his flat convinced that he will soon be picked up by the Thought Police. Any escape from life under the regime of the Party seems impossible.

In and out of the dark . . . their mothers Notice how the structure of the sentence, with its frequent use of 'and', reinforces the idea of astonishing numbers of people.

People were shooting . . . one movement Here the use of verbs, particularly those of one syllable, reinforces the impression of haste.

sawdust When Orwell was writing, floors of bars were frequently sprinkled with sawdust to soak up spilt beer, etc.

altercation Dispute.

bleeding Euphemism for 'bloody', frequently used for rhythmic effect only.

February your grandmother! An expression of disbelief.

anodyne Pain-killing drug (used here figuratively).

I arst you . . . didn't I? All of the old man's speeches are written by Orwell in an attempt to represent cockney dialect.

boozer Slang term for 'public house'.

donkey's years ago Colloquial term meaning 'a very long time ago'.

Salvation Army A religious organization on a military model, founded by William Booth (1829–1912).

Boat-Race night The night following the annual boat race on the River Thames between two crews from Oxford and Cambridge Universities.

No truck No dealings.

Immediately above his head . . . been gilded This was the customary sign above a pawnbroker's shop, and is rarely seen today. People left personal articles with the pawnbroker who then loaned them a sum of money. Upon repayment of the loan and interest, the pawnbroker returned the articles.

His voice was soft . . . majority of proles A hint that Mr Charrington is not what he seems.

lacquered Covered with a coloured varnish made of shellac and alcohol.

As Winston wandered . . . picked it up Notice the metaphorical use of 'caught' in this sentence. His attraction to the paperweight, an object from the past, leads him eventually to rent the upstairs room from Mr Charrington, with disastrous results for Julia and himself.

There's another room . . . going upstairs Notice how gently Winston is led into a trap by Mr Charrington in this speech and those following.

There's no telescreen! See note on 'The great majority . . .' in Part One, Chapter 7.

The frame's fixed . . . I dare say Coming back to this comment when we have read the book once, we have to admire Mr Charrington's audacity when he appears to be willing to sell Winston the picture concealing the telescreen. See Part Two, Chapter 9, p.176.

That was a rhyme we had . . . and caught you This is a factual description of the nursery rhyme, but it carries sinister overtones in view of the capture of Winston and Julia later in the book (Part Two, Chapter 9, pp.176–9). The complete text of the rhyme can be found in *The Oxford Nursery Rhyme Book*, assembled by Iona and Peter Opie, published in 1955.

reconnoitring Assessing the strategic features of a place.

The lump of glass . . . away The glass paperweight develops great symbolic importance in connection with Winston's relationship with Julia. Notice how he immediately becomes conscious of its weight as soon as he has been seen by her when leaving the shop. See also Part Two, Chapter 4, p.112 and pp.119–20, and Part Two, Chapter 9, pp.177–8.

lassitude Weariness.

in the torture chamber Points forward significantly to Part Three of the novel.

He tried to think of O'Brien . . . him away Note the coupling of O'Brien and the Thought Police in Winston's mind. This is ironic in view of later events.

knell This can mean either the sound of a bell rung after a death, or, figuratively, something regarded as an omen of death. Orwell most likely intended both meanings to be understood, particularly in view of the emphasis on bells in the nursery rhyme earlier in the chapter.

Revision questions on Part One

1 Describe, as fully as possible, Winston's actions on returning to his flat on the day that he begins his diary.

2 Write a brief description of the Two Minutes Hate which Winston remembers in Chapter 1.

3 What impression does Orwell convey of the Parsons children? How does their mother react to them?

4 Give an account of Winston's dream in Chapter 3 before he gets up to take part in Physical Jerks.

5 Describe briefly (a) Syme and (b) Parsons.

6 Show how Katharine's reactions to Winston reflect the Party's attitude towards sex.

7 Explain the importance of the photograph of Jones, Aaronson and Rutherford which once came into Winston's possession.

8 Why does Winston feel frustrated by his conversation with the old man in the prole pub?

9 Write a close description of the room over Mr Charrington's shop.

10 Describe Winston's feelings on seeing the girl from the Fiction Department when he leaves the junk-shop.

Part Two

Chapter 1

Winston leaves his work to go to the lavatory and meets the dark-haired girl in a corridor. One of her arms is in a sling and she falls to the ground in front of him. As he helps her up the girl slips a note into Winston's hand, which he manages to read when he returns to his work. He is amazed to discover that the message reads 'I love you'. Winston wishes to arrange a meeting with the girl, but has to wait several days until he is able to sit near her in the canteen. They eat their meal in apparent silence, but the girl is able to give him instructions to meet her in a crowd in Victory Square after work. When Winston sees her in the square, a convoy carrying Eurasian prisoners passes by, which everyone runs to see. Under cover of watching the prisoners go by the girl gives Winston directions to a meeting place for the following Sunday afternoon.

'roughed in' Outlined in rough.

his intellect . . . meant death In a sense this proves to be the case, as Winston is caught with Julia and taken to the Ministry of Love.

papier-mâché Moulded paper pulp.

under a cloud Out of favour, discredited.

He thought of her . . . in his dream See Part One, Chapter 3, p.28.

mated Finally defeated.

For the messages . . . that were inapplicable Orwell may have been thinking of similar postcards issued to troops during the Second World War at times when severe censorship of information sent home was deemed necessary.

It was impossible . . . in real life This thought is to prove true.

fluted Having semi-cylindrical vertical grooves.

at the top . . . Airstrip One In 1984 Big Brother's statue has
replaced that of Nelson in the renamed Trafalgar Square.
scrimmage Tussle, confused struggle.
callouses Pads of hard skin.
With hands locked . . . of hair Orwell skilfully draws a link
between the aged prisoner and the lovers, in such a way as to
indicate that their hands, locked together in affection, will one
day be bound together as his have been in the past.

Chapter 2

Winston has made his way to the country meeting-place
described by the dark-haired girl. He is picking bluebells when
she arrives and leads him to a secret clearing in a wood. They
embrace and the girl tells Winston that her name is Julia. She
reveals that she is against all that the Party stands for. They
walk to the edge of the wood where Winston sees a landscape
which matches the Golden Country of his dreams. The couple
listen to a thrush singing and on returning to the clearing they
make love, after Julia has told Winston that she is corrupt to
the bones, which pleases him since he believes that in-
discriminate physical desire is the force which will overthrow
the Party.

Winston picked his way . . . ring-doves Notice the emphasis on
nature. See also note on 'the Golden Country' in Part One,
Chapter 3.
wooden-seated During the Second World War seats on public
transport in Britain were frequently unpadded in order to save
materials vital to the war effort.
black-market butter Butter obtained illegally in excess of one's
allotted ration.

A hand fell . . . the girl Orwell maintains tension here by means of the paragraph break and the succeeding short sentences.

etiolated Pale and unhealthy-looking through lack of exposure to natural light.

The first whiff . . . troubling See Part Two, Chapter 7, pp.130–33.

obeisance Gesture of respect or salutation.

virtuosity Skill (particularly in performance of music).

This time . . . difficulty i.e. he was not impotent, as he had been when they first embraced (p.99).

Chapter 3

Julia gives Winston a different route by which to return home, and leaves separately after arranging to meet him later in the week in a crowded open market where they may be able to talk in safety. They find it difficult to meet during the month of May because of their long hours of work and commitment to so-called 'voluntary' activities for the Party. However, they manage to have one afternoon together in the belfry of a ruined church, during which time Julia tells Winston about her background and work in the Fiction Department at the Ministry of Truth. She informs him about her love affairs and in turn he tells her about his marriage to the frigid Katharine. The chapter concludes with Julia indicating that she does not totally share Winston's view that they are doomed because they have set themselves against the Party.

bloody In this context this means irritating, infuriating.

it was inconceivable . . . indoors. At this stage Winston has not seriously considered renting the room over Mr Charrington's shop.

Winston's working week . . . even longer Once again Orwell is relating events to those he knew himself. Very long working hours were usual for civilians during the Second World War.

She described to him . . . round him Cf. Part One, Chapter 6, p.57.

sexual privation Lack of sexual contact.

loosestrife A wild plant. The purple variety is common in ditches and on river banks, while the narrow-leaved loosestrife is to be found on damp, bare ground.

We are the dead Winston's statement has been foreshadowed earlier (Part One, Chapter 7, p.64), and points forward to its use by O'Brien (Part Two, Chapter 8, p.143), and to the chilling variation 'You are the dead' from the telescreen in Part Two, Chapter 9, p.176.

Chapter 4

In spite of his realization of the danger of capture by the Thought Police, Winston has rented the room above Mr Charrington's shop. He is waiting there one evening for Julia. In the yard below the window a prole woman is singing while she pegs out babies' napkins on a clothesline. When Julia arrives she brings with her black-market provisions and makes herself up with cosmetics obtained from a shop in the proletarian quarters. Winston and Julia go to bed and fall asleep. When they wake up Julia throws a shoe at a rat which she sees in a hole in the wainscoting. Winston reveals that rats are his greatest horror, and Julia says that she will block up the hole. They have coffee and Julia examines the contents of the room including the paperweight and the engraving of St Clement Dane's Church, revealing that she knows part of the nursery

Woman

Rats

Paper/wght.

rhyme in which the latter figures. Winston lies looking into the paperweight, feeling that he and Julia are enclosed within it, together with the objects in the room.

bolster A long stuffed pillow, usually placed under other pillows on a bed.

In the corner . . . half-darkness The paperweight can be said to represent the relationship between Winston and Julia. Their love blossoms while they believe themselves to be hidden from the Thought Police, and the paperweight gleams in the half-darkness. See also Part Two, Chapter 9, pp.177–8.

fender A low frame, usually made of metal, placed round a fire to prevent live coals from rolling into the room. However, at Mr Charrington's there is no coal fire, merely an oilstove.

gratuitous Unwarranted, motiveless.

It was only . . . 'cart awye! The prole woman's song acts as an ironic counterpoint to the love affair between Winston and Julia, which is in truth a hopeless fancy.

It's started . . . time i.e. her monthly period.

Don't go . . . the window Because he might be seen from outside.

Her voice floated . . . sing about In writing about the prole woman Orwell may have been remembering a passage in his wartime diary for 10 June 1942, in which he describes the charwomen at the BBC, where he was working: 'They sit in the reception hall waiting for their brooms to be issued to them and making as much noise as a parrot house, and then they have wonderful choruses, all singing together as they sweep the passages.'

As he took her . . . cavernous mouth See Part One, Chapter 6, pp.55–8.

rouge A fine red powder used for colouring cheeks.

wainscoting Wooden boarding on the lower part of the wall of a room.

Of all horrors . . . a rat! Presumably, in the light of later events (Part Three, Chapter 5, pp.227–30), Winston's words are picked up by the telescreen operators.

countersign Password given to a man on guard, or by which members of a secret society may recognize each other.

I bet that picture's . . . behind it Julia is referring to the
possibility of bed bugs behind the picture. However, Orwell may
have intended her statement to convey a double meaning without
her being aware of the fact. The word 'bug', meaning concealed
microphone, was first used in print in America in 1946, according
to *A Supplement to the Oxford English Dictionary, Volume 1, A–G*,
edited by R. W. Burchfield (1972).

The paperweight . . . of the crystal However, see Part Two,
Chapter 9, p.177: 'The fragment of coral, a tiny crinkle of pink
like a sugar rosebud from a cake, rolled across the mat. How
small, thought Winston, how small it always was!'

Chapter 5

As Winston had foreseen, Syme vanishes, presumably to be
vaporized. Preparations for Hate Week keep the staff of all the
Ministries extremely busy, while in the evenings Parsons or-
ganizes the decoration of Victory Mansions with bunting.
Winston and Julia meet when they can in their secret room,
and sometimes Mr Charrington shows Winston items from the
past and repeats fragments of nursery rhymes to him. The
lovers are aware that they cannot hope to survive for long, but
they discuss the possibility of active rebellion against the Party.
Winston realizes that Julia is in some ways more perceptive
than himself, but he is shocked to learn how her memory of the
truth about the never-ending war has been eroded by Party
propaganda. Julia has little interest in the methods used by the
Party to present itself as always being right.

Syme . . . had never existed Winston had foreseen Syme's
disappearance in Part One, Chapter 5, p.46.
vestibule Lobby.

effigies Images made to represent particular people.

atrocity pamphlets Pamphlets dealing with cruel and wicked acts alleged to have been committed by a nation's military enemies.

febrile Feverish.

He was . . . native element He was in the atmosphere and surroundings which he liked best.

acrid Bitter, pungent.

As though to harmonize . . . blown to pieces Orwell is here drawing on memories of the air raids on London in the 1940s.

As soon as they arrived . . . the black market In order to prevent the bugs becoming active.

inviolate Unprofaned, here meaning sacred to Winston and Julia alone.

pocket Isolated area.

pinchbeck An alloy of copper and zinc resembling gold in appearance.

mythology Here meaning lies presented as historical truth.

every statue . . . been altered Compare the situation in Russia since the Revolution. For example, Petrograd had its name changed to Leningrad in 1924, while Tsaritsyn became known as Stalingrad in 1925. However, following the denunciation of Stalin, the latter town was renamed Volgograd in 1961.

Chapter 6

Winston is walking down a corridor at the Ministry when he becomes aware that someone is following him. It is O'Brien, who begins a conversation with him about his Newspeak articles in *The Times*. O'Brien offers to lend Winston an advance copy of the tenth edition of the Newspeak Dictionary and gives him his address, asking him to call and collect the book when it is convenient. It seems evident to Winston that O'Brien is inviting him to join a conspiracy against the Party. He knows that he will call at O'Brien's flat at some time in the future, even though the logical outcome of his rebellion against the Party is torture and probable death in the Ministry of Love.

I was talking . . . expert Ironic. Winston believes that O'Brien is taking a risk by referring to Syme, whereas he probably talked to him during interrogation at the Ministry of Love.

immediately seeing . . . tended i.e. that O'Brien is about to arrange for him to see a copy of Goldstein's book.

leather-covered . . . ink-pencil As a member of the Inner Party, O'Brien possesses luxury objects.

which this time . . . conceal In contrast to the occasion when Julia slipped him her note (Part Two, Chapter 1, p.88).

directories Books listing addresses, telephone numbers, names of householders, etc.

The last step . . . Love But Winston does not realize that this will involve O'Brien so directly.

Chapter 7

Winston wakes up in distress from a dream in which he remembered his last glimpse of his mother. He recalls conditions prior to her disappearance, in particular the hunger and deprivation which everyone suffered. Winston remembers the squalid room in which he lived with his mother and ailing sister, and the way in which he always demanded more than his fair share of food. One day he had stolen his sister's share of a chocolate ration and run outside. When he returned his mother and sister had disappeared and he was sent to a colony for homeless children. Winston tells Julia about his dream, realizing that the Party has done its best to destroy natural feelings between human beings. He believes that only the proles have stayed human. The chapter ends with Winston and Julia discussing what will happen when the Thought Police eventually capture them, and agreeing that although confession is inevitable the Party cannot get inside the human heart.

the Jewish woman . . . to pieces See Part One, Chapter 1, pp.10–11.

the gangs of youths . . . colour Brings to mind the Blackshirts (followers of the British Fascist leader, Sir Oswald Mosley), who were active in the East End of London in the 1930s.

lay-figure A jointed wooden figure of the human body on which artists display clothes or drapery.

simian Monkey-like.

It was perfectly . . . camp Notice the force of 'merely' in this sentence.

His mind . . . darkening water See Part One, Chapter 3, p.27.

And in thinking . . . cabbage-stalk See Part One, Chapter 8, p.69.

Perhaps that was . . . their hands An ominous pointer to the events of Part Three.

Chapter 8

Winston and Julia go to O'Brien's flat to collect the dictionary. When they are admitted into O'Brien's presence he is working, and Winston wonders whether he has made a mistake in thinking that O'Brien is a conspirator. However, he turns off the telescreen and makes them welcome, offering them wine in which to drink a toast to Goldstein. O'Brien asks Winston what he is prepared to do to overthrow the Party, and describes the organization of the Brotherhood. Julia leaves separately and O'Brien arranges to let Winston have a copy of Goldstein's book in the near future.

The whole atmosphere . . . intimidating Notice the contrast with the description of Victory Mansions at the beginning of the book (Part One, Chapter 1, p.5).

demur Objection.

equivocal Ambiguous, capable of more than one interpretation.

founded on a dream See Part One, Chapter 2, pp.23–4.

valet A gentleman's servant whose chief function is to look after clothes, etc.

catechism Mode of instruction by means of question and answer. The word is frequently found in a religious context.

You are prepared . . . murder? See Part Three, Chapter 3, p.217, where O'Brien plays a recording of this conversation to Winston.

disseminate Spread, sow.

We may be obliged . . . different O'Brien's words carry a terrible irony, since Winston's treatment in the Ministry of Love makes him into a physical wreck. See Part Three, Chapter 3, pp.217–19.

synthetic Artificially formed, i.e. by means of plastic surgery.

I shall . . . different person Ironic in view of O'Brien's role as Winston's interrogator in Part Three.

persiflage Light irony, banter.

When you looked . . . defeated Again ironic in view of what happens in Part Three.

stratagem Trick, manoeuvre.

we are occasionally . . . cell i.e. to enable him to commit suicide.

We are the dead See note on 'We are the dead' in Part Two, Chapter 3.

handfuls of dust Recalls line 30 of T. S. Eliot's *The Waste Land* (1922): 'I will show you fear in a handful of dust'.

later we will arrange ... you This points forward ominously to events in Part Three, but Winston fails to notice the hidden significance of O'Brien's remark.

In the place ... no darkness See Part One, Chapter 2, pp.23–4, and Part Three, Chapter 1, p.184.

You knew ... last line In fact O'Brien merely completes the stanza, not the whole rhyme. See note on 'That was a rhyme we had . . .' in Part One, Chapter 8, concerning the significance of the nursery rhyme in connection with the relationship between Winston and Julia.

Chapter 9

Winston makes his way to the room over Mr Charrington's shop, carrying with him a briefcase containing Goldstein's book. He is exhausted after having worked more than ninety hours in five days. He reaches the shop before Julia and begins to read the book. When Julia arrives they go to bed and Winston reads more of Goldstein's book aloud to her, but after a time she falls asleep. Winston puts the book down and also goes to sleep. When they awake they observe the woman noticed on an earlier occasion (Part Two, Chapter 4) pegging out washing in the yard below, and Winston's conviction that the future belongs to the proles is reinforced. Winston and Julia are then interrupted by a voice from a concealed tele-screen and the room is invaded by armed guards. Julia is punched in the solar plexus and carried away while Winston stands rigid with fear. Mr Charrington enters the room and Winston realizes that he is in fact a member of the Thought Police.

lymph A colourless alkaline fluid contained in tissues and organs of the body, resembling blood without the red corpuscles.

debauch A bout of over-indulgence in something.

irrationally convinced . . . with him In this chapter Orwell emphasizes that Winston feels that he is safe (see also p.173), yet this is to be the day of his capture by the Thought Police.

caterpillars Articulated, unbroken steel tracks which pass round the wheels of tanks, enabling them to progress across rough ground.

Rumpelstiltskin A deformed dwarf in a German folk tale.

feral Wild, brutal.

switched from one line Changed from one political point of view.

Mattresses were brought up . . . canteen Orwell is once again relating events to conditions that existed in the Second World War, when pressure of work in government departments sometimes forced people to sleep in their offices.

although the water . . . tepid Another indication of the uncomfortable conditions prevailing in 1984.

equilibrium State of balance.

fecundity Fertility.

synthesize Produce artificially.

empirical Based on observation and experiment, as opposed to theory.

hierarchical society A society organized into classes ranged one above the next.

logistics The branch of strategy concerned with the movement and quartering of troops.

The effect was to convince . . . sooner or later Compare the situation with that which exists in the world today.

If he were allowed contact . . . evaporate Here and on p.166 Orwell is describing conditions which currently exist in many Communist countries, principally Russia and China.

tenets Principles, doctrines.

ruminant Cud-chewing.

totalitarian Relating to forms of government which permit no rival parties or policies and demand total subservience of the individual to the state.

A Party member lives . . . to be detected It is ironic that Winston feels safe while reading these lines. Later in the novel (Part Three, Chapter 3, p.210) O'Brien tells him that he collaborated in writing Goldstein's book. In effect, in this section Winston is being told very clearly that he is trapped.

analogies Similarities, parallelisms.

ossified Became rigid.

He understood *how* . . . understood *why* This links with Winston's diary entry in Part One, Chapter 7, p.67, and also points forward to Part Three, Chapter 3, p.210.

sanity is not statistical Contrasts this statement with Winston's later reflection in the Ministry of Love (Part Three, Chapter 4, p.222).

We are the dead See note on 'We are the dead' in Part Two, Chapter 3.

a thin, cultivated voice . . . before See note on 'His voice was soft' in Part One, Chapter 8.

Someone had picked up . . . hearth-stone See note on 'The paperweight . . .' in Part Two, Chapter 4.

Winston had a glimpse . . . hit him yet Note Orwell's skilful use of the semi-colon, the paragraph break and short sentences to emphasize finality and suspense.

Revision questions on Part Two

1 What difficulties are experienced by Winston in arranging a meeting with Julia after she has slipped him the note?

2 Explain why Winston wishes to know about Julia's past sexual experience when they make love for the first time.

3 Why does Julia encourage Winston to volunteer for munition work on one evening a week?

4 Describe Winston's reactions when Julia catches sight of a rat in the room over the junk-shop.

5 Write a brief summary of the preparations for Hate Week which are described in Chapter 5.

6 Describe O'Brien's attitude when he meets Winston in the corridor and promises to lend him the Newspeak Dictionary.

7 Write a detailed account of the behaviour of Winston as a child when he was living in one room with his mother and sister, as he recalls it in Chapter 7.

8 Describe Winston's feelings towards O'Brien when he and Julia visit his flat in Chapter 8.

9 Give an account of the reactions of the crowd at the Hate Week demonstration when it becomes known that Eastasia and not Eurasia is the enemy.

10 Describe briefly events in the room over Mr Charrington's shop from the moment that Winston and Julia first hear the voice from the telescreen.

Part Three

Chapter 1

Winston is in a cell at the Ministry of Love. While he is waiting to see what happens to him, other prisoners are brought into the cell, including the poet Ampleforth, and Parsons, whose small daughter has denounced him for thoughtcrime. Several prisoners are consigned to Room 101, although the full significance of this is not evident at this stage. Time passes and Winston, who has not been fed, feels increasingly unwell. He thinks of Julia and believes that if he could save her by doubling his own pain he would do so. The door of the cell opens and O'Brien enters accompanied by a guard. Winston realizes that he has allowed himself to be deceived by O'Brien, who is really a loyal member of the Inner Party. The chapter ends with Winston being attacked by the guard.

shouted down the telescreen Made so much noise that it could not be heard.

place with no darkness See Part One, Chapter 2, pp.23–4 and Part Two, Chapter 8, p.145.

Kipling Rudyard Kipling (1865–1936) was an English novelist, poet and short-story writer who was awarded the Nobel Prize for Literature in 1907.

desultorily In a disconnected fashion.

going off the rails i.e. departing from the Party line.

The man looked frantically . . . own place Orwell includes this episode to foreshadow Winston's conduct in Room 101. (See Part Three, Chapter 5, p.230.)

Chapter 2

Winston is lying immobile undergoing interrogation. He is unable to tell how long it has been since his ordeal began. Physical violence has been followed by mental torture, causing him to confess to a long list of imaginary crimes in an attempt to avoid further pain. Winston is aware that O'Brien is directing operations, but nevertheless feels drawn to him. O'Brien reveals that he has been watching Winston for seven years and explains that he is going to 'reclaim' him. When Winston will not agree that the Party can make two and two equal five, if it wishes, he is again tortured. O'Brien explains to him why the Party cannot allow opposition, and tells him that no one is spared who has once gone astray. The chapter ends with O'Brien allowing Winston to question him. He learns that Julia has betrayed him, and when he asks what is in Room 101 receives the sardonic reply that everyone knows the answer to that question.

prevaricate Speak misleadingly.

hallucination Illusion, apparent perception of an object not present in reality.

metaphysician A person who speculates on the nature of truth and existence.

Do you remember . . . make four? See note on 'In the end the Party . . .' in Part One, Chapter 7.

exaltation Rapture, elation.

Never again will you . . . ourselves This is one of the most horrifying sections of the book. The negation of all that is human contained in O'Brien's words is more appalling than the physical tortures inflicted on Winston.

You see now . . . any rate possible i.e. to think in the way demanded by the Party.

ampoule A sealed capsule or phial containing one dose of a drug.

Did not the statement . . . absurdity? Because a person who
did not exist could not be addressed directly.

There was a trace . . . Room 101 The horrors in store for
Winston are emphasized by Orwell's use of 'trace of amusement',
'ironical gleam' and 'drily'.

Chapter 3

O'Brien tells Winston that there are three stages in his reintegration – learning, understanding, and acceptance – and
that he is about to enter on the second stage. He informs him
that he himself collaborated in writing the book supposed to
have been written by Goldstein, and that the proles will never
revolt. In his efforts to re-educate Winston, O'Brien submits
him to questioning, inflicting pain on him when he is unable to
give the required answers. He reveals that the Party seeks
power entirely for its own sake, and when Winston claims to be
morally superior to the Party, demonstrates the hollowness of
his assertion by playing back to him a recording of the assur-
ances he gave when he wished to join the Brotherhood (Part
Two, Chapter 8). O'Brien then humiliates Winston further by
forcing him to look at his broken, naked body in a mirror.
Winston weeps, but comforts himself slightly by telling
O'Brien that he has not betrayed Julia.

You foresaw yourself . . . would say Remember that Winston
was not able to complete reading *the book*, but knew that
Goldstein's final message must be that if there was hope it lay in
the proles. (See Part Two, Chapter 9, p.175.)

oligarchies States governed by small exclusive groups of people.

The weariness . . . organism O'Brien is putting forward the
view that the healthiness of the Party can be demonstrated by the

tiredness of individuals who have spent their entire lives working in its service.

mammoths and mastodons Large extinct animals of the elephant family.

light-years A light-year is the distance light travels in a year, about six million million miles.

hedonistic Adjective related to hedonism, the doctrine that pleasure is the chief good.

Winston had tried to shrink . . . bed again Notice how Winston's physical movements reflect his reactions to O'Brien's arguments in this chapter. Earlier (p.212), he tried to struggle into a sitting position. However, when he senses defeat at this point and on p.214, he shrinks back upon the bed.

This drama . . . subtler forms We learned earlier that O'Brien had been watching Winston for seven years (Part Three, Chapter 2, p.196).

malleable Adaptable, pliable.

Two other voices . . . face See Part Two, Chapter 8, p.140.

O'Brien made . . . making By playing back the recording, O'Brien has proved to Winston that he has no right to feel morally superior.

O'Brien looked . . . thoughtfully Note the force of 'thoughtfully' in this sentence. O'Brien sees the need for Winston to betray Julia if he is to be broken completely.

Chapter 4

Time has passed and Winston's living conditions are now more comfortable. When he becomes physically stronger he begins the task of making himself accept the Party's views of reality, but finds it hard to operate doublethink. He wonders how long the Party will keep him alive before shooting him.

He has a vision of Julia which causes him to call her name aloud, and is aware that he will have been overheard by the guards who will realize that he is not really trying to re-educate himself. Finally he is confronted by O'Brien, who send him to Room 101.

He was much better Notice how this opening sentence gives us false hope for Winston.

torpid Inactive, sluggish.

Even the speck . . . replaced See Part One, Chapter 2, p.26.

Yes, even . . . Presumably some of the photographs were of Winston and Julia having sexual intercourse.

Sanity was statistical Contrast with Winston's earlier assertion in Part Two, Chapter 9, p.173.

The pencil felt . . . fingers An interesting contrast with an earlier occasion in the novel when Winston is shown writing in his diary. Then his 'pen had slid voluptuously over the smooth paper' (Part One, Chapter 1, p.18) as he wrote DOWN WITH BIG BROTHER. Now that he is trying to re-educate himself his awkwardness is emphasized.

Chapter 5

In Room 101 Winston is strapped tightly in a chair facing two small tables. O'Brien enters and tells him that Room 101 contains the worst thing in the world, which in his case happens to be rats. Meanwhile a guard has brought in a cage containing two large rats, and O'Brien shows Winston how it can be strapped against his face in such a way that the animals will be able to savage him. Winston panics, and, in an endeavour to save himself, screams that Julia should be tortured in his place.

This place . . . possible to go Note the appropriate location of Room 101. Winston is to be forced to face what he most fears, in fact to go 'as deep down as it was possible to go' within himself.

But he hardly . . . surroundings Orwell conveys Winston's anxiety to the reader by the brevity of this sentence, and the way it is separated from the one which precedes it.

baize A coarse woollen material.

impalement Transfixing upon a stake.

In your case . . . rats See note on 'Of all horrors . . . a rat!' in Part Two, Chapter 4.

They were enormous rats Note the way in which Winston's horror is concentrated in this one brief sentence.

He must interpose . . . rats See note on 'The man looked frantically . . . own place' in Part Three, Chapter 1.

an old scaly . . . air Orwell increases the horror at this point by personifying the rat.

didactically As though teaching someone a lesson.

Chapter 6

Winston has been released from the Ministry of Love, and is sitting in the Chestnut Tree Café, where he is a regular customer. He has become a heavy drinker both at home and at the café. Oceania is once more at war with Eurasia, and news of an important military engagement is expected shortly over the telescreen. Winston recalls a chance meeting with Julia when they each revealed that they had betrayed the other. Their love for one another has been completely destroyed by their experiences in the Ministry of Love, and neither of them showed signs of wishing to take up their relationship again, even though it would now have been allowed by the Party.

Winston then remembers a happy childhood afternoon spent playing snakes and ladders with his mother, watched by his little sister. However, since he has now been almost totally re-educated by the Party, he pushes the memory from his mind, just as the telescreen announces a great victory over Eurasia. Winston is caught up in the mass excitement, and realizes that the final stage of his reintegration is complete, and that he now loves Big Brother.

Winston sat . . . Victory Gin Winston is now in the same position as Jones, Aaronson and Rutherford when he remembered seeing them in the Chestnut Tree (Part One, Chapter 7, pp.64–5). Compare the two descriptions for close verbal echoes.

A Eurasian army . . . speed Notice that political alignments have changed once again since Winston was in the Ministry of Love.

since nobody cared . . . to him Compare Part One, Chapter 7, p.64: 'It was not wise even to be seen in the neighbourhood of such people.'

They can't get inside . . . said See Part Two, Chapter 7, p.136.

It was in the Park . . . wind Notice the way in which the weather matches the mood of the meeting between Winston and Julia.

grizzled Whimpered, cried fretfully.

It was a false memory i.e. under the new thought processes that the 're-educated' Winston has learned. In fact, the memory was true.

the final, indispensable, healing change i.e. acceptance, the third stage in the reintegration process outlined to Winston by O'Brien (Part Three, Chapter 3, p.209).

Revision questions on Part Three

1 What reasons are given by (a) Ampleforth and (b) Parsons for being sent to the Ministry of Love?

2 Describe Winston's first reactions when O'Brien enters his cell in Chapter 1.

3 What reasons does O'Brien give for interrogating Winston when it is the Party's intention to destroy him no matter what happens?

4 Describe O'Brien's reactions when Winston wishes to know what is in Room 101.

5 List the three stages in Winston's reintegration, as stated by O'Brien.

6 Why, according to O'Brien, does the Party seek power?

7 Why does O'Brien force Winston to strip and look at himself in a three-sided mirror?

8 Describe Winston's state of mind when he is faced by his greatest horror in Room 101.

9 Do you feel more sympathy for (a) Winston or (b) Julia when they meet in the Park? Give reasons for your answer.

10 Describe Winston's feelings on hearing the victory announcement on the telescreen at the Chestnut Tree Café.

Appendix – The Principles of Newspeak

The subject matter of the appendix is dealt with earlier in this book, prior to the textual notes.

devotees Persons devoted to a cause, faith, etc.
staccato Abrupt, detached.
ipso facto By that very fact.
euphemisms Mild or vague words or expressions substituted for harsh realities, e.g. 'rodent operative' for 'rat catcher', 'made reduntant' for 'dismissed'.
Agitprop System of Russian propaganda.
Karl Marx German Socialist (1818–63), co-author with Friedrich Engels of *The Communist Manifesto* (1848), the basic document of Communist theory.
Paris Commune Term applied to the usurping committee or government which held power during the Reign of Terror in the French Revolution, and also to the communalistic body which governed in Paris in 1871 after its evacuation by the Germans.
inimical to Hostile to, harmful to.
panegyric Expression of praise, eulogy.

General questions

1 Summarize the plot of *Nineteen Eighty-Four* in about forty lines.

2 Discuss the importance of the backgrounds and settings in the novel.

3 Winston has been described as the only fully developed character in *Nineteen Eighty-Four*. Do you agree with this view, and, if so, does it constitute a weakness in the novel?

4 Discuss the ways in which Orwell makes his descriptions of the work carried out by Winston and Julia in the Ministry of Truth interesting.

5 Trace the development of the different stages of Winston's attitude towards Julia in the course of the book.

6 What is the importance of the proles in *Nineteen Eighty-Four*? Refer closely to two characters or episodes in your answer.

7 Consider the part played by any two of the following characters in *Nineteen Eighty-Four*: Parsons, Syme, Ampleforth, Mr Charrington.

8 Examine the significance in the novel of Winston's memories of his childhood and marriage.

9 'On the whole we feel no particular attraction for Winston or Julia. We are interested in the nature of their revolt.' Consider this quotation, giving reasons for your reactions to it.

10 It has been said that 'We know throughout the book that the Party will defeat Winston.' Despite the probable accuracy of this statement, show how Orwell maintains suspense in *Nineteen Eighty-Four*.

11 Some critics have found the section in Room 101 unsatisfactory, one even going so far as to write that 'the idea of

Room 101 and the rats will always remain comic rather than horrific.' Discuss your own reactions to the episode.

12 The extracts from Goldstein's book and the Appendix on *The Principles of Newspeak* have been criticized as inappropriate for inclusion within a novel. What is your opinion?

13 Discuss the character and function of O'Brien in *Nineteen Eighty-Four*.

14 Consider the effectiveness of Orwell's use of symbolism in *Nineteen Eighty-Four*.

15 Orwell has been quoted as saying of *Nineteen Eighty-Four*, 'It wouldn't have been so gloomy if I hadn't been so ill.' Would the book have been so effective if it had not ended so pessimistically?

Pan study aids Titles published in the Brodie's Notes series

W. H. Auden Selected Poetry

Jane Austen Emma Mansfield Park Northanger Abbey Persuasion
Pride and Prejudice

Anthologies of Poetry Ten Twentieth Century Poets
The Metaphysical Poets The Poet's Tale

Samuel Beckett Waiting for Godot

Arnold Bennett The Old Wives' Tale

William Blake Songs of Innocence and Experience

Robert Bolt A Man for All Seasons

Harold Brighouse Hobson's Choice

Charlotte Brontë Jane Eyre

Emily Brontë Wuthering Heights

Robert Browning Selected Poetry

John Bunyan The Pilgrim's Progress

Geoffrey Chaucer (parallel texts editions) The Franklin's Tale
The Knight's Tale The Miller's Tale The Nun's Priest's Tale
The Pardoner's Tale Prologue to the Canterbury Tales
The Wife of Bath's Tale

Richard Church Over the Bridge

John Clare Selected Poetry and Prose

Samuel Taylor Coleridge Selected Poetry and Prose

Wilkie Collins The Woman in White

William Congreve The Way of the World

Joseph Conrad The Nigger of the Narcissus & Youth
The Secret Agent

Charles Dickens Bleak House David Copperfield Dombey and Son
Great Expectations Hard Times Little Dorrit Oliver Twist
Our Mutual Friend A Tale of Two Cities

Gerald Durrell My Family and Other Animals

George Eliot Middlemarch The Mill on the Floss Silas Marner

T. S. Eliot Murder in the Cathedral Selected Poems

J. G. Farrell The Siege of Krishnapur

Henry Fielding Joseph Andrews

F. Scott Fitzgerald The Great Gatsby

E. M. Forster Howards End A Passage to India
Where Angels Fear to Tread

William Golding Lord of the Flies The Spire

Oliver Goldsmith Two Plays of Goldsmith: She Stoops to Conquer;
The Good Natured Man

Graham Greene Brighton Rock The Power and the Glory
The Quiet American

Thom Gunn and Ted Hughes Selected Poems

Thomas Hardy Chosen Poems of Thomas Hardy Far from the
Madding Crowd Jude the Obscure The Mayor of Casterbridge
Return of the Native Tess of the D'Urbervilles The Trumpet-Major

L. P. Hartley The Go-Between The Shrimp and the Anemone

Joseph Heller Catch-22

Ernest Hemingway For Whom the Bell Tolls
The Old Man and the Sea

Barry Hines A Kestrel for a Knave

Gerard Manley Hopkins Poetry and Prose of Gerard Manley
Hopkins

Aldous Huxley Brave New World

Henry James Washington Square

Ben Jonson The Alchemist Volpone

James Joyce A Portrait of the Artist as a Young Man

John Keats Selected Poems and Letters of John Keats

Ken Kesey One Flew Over the Cuckoo's Nest

Rudyard Kipling Kim

D. H. Lawrence The Rainbow Selected Tales Sons and Lovers

Harper Lee To Kill a Mocking-bird

Laurie Lee As I Walked out One Midsummer Morning
Cider with Rosie

Thomas Mann Death in Venice & Tonio Kröger

Christopher Marlowe Doctor Faustus Edward the Second

W. Somerset Maugham Of Human Bondage

Arthur Miller The Crucible Death of a Salesman

John Milton A Choice of Milton's Verse Comus and Samson
Agonistes Paradise Lost, I, II

Sean O'Casey Juno and the Paycock The Shadow of a Gunman and
The Plough and the Stars

George Orwell Animal Farm 1984

John Osborne Luther
Alexander Pope Selected Poetry
Siegfried Sassoon Memoirs of a Fox-Hunting Man
Peter Shaffer The Royal Hunt of the Sun
William Shakespeare Antony and Cleopatra As You Like It
Coriolanus Hamlet Henry IV (Part I) Henry IV (Part II) Henry V
Julius Caesar King Lear King Richard III Love's Labour's Lost
Macbeth Measure for Measure The Merchant of Venice
A Midsummer Night's Dream Much Ado about Nothing Othello
Richard II Romeo and Juliet The Sonnets The Taming of the Shrew
The Tempest Twelfth Night The Winter's Tale
G. B. Shaw Androcles and the Lion Arms and the Man
Caesar and Cleopatra The Doctor's Dilemma Pygmalion Saint Joan
Richard Sheridan Plays of Sheridan: The Rivals; The Critic;
The School for Scandal
John Steinbeck The Grapes of Wrath Of Mice and Men & The
Pearl
Tom Stoppard Rosencrantz and Guildenstern are Dead
J. M. Synge The Playboy of the Western World
Jonathan Swift Gulliver's Travels
Alfred Tennyson Selected Poetry
William Thackeray Vanity Fair
Flora Thompson Lark Rise to Candleford
Dylan Thomas Under Milk Wood
Anthony Trollope Barchester Towers
Mark Twain Huckleberry Finn
Keith Waterhouse Billy Liar
Evelyn Waugh Decline and Fall Scoop
H. G. Wells The History of Mr Polly
John Webster The White Devil
Oscar Wilde The Importance of Being Earnest
Virginia Woolf To the Lighthouse
William Wordsworth The Prelude (Books 1, 2)
John Wyndham The Chrysalids
W. B. Yeats Selected Poetry

Australian Titles
George Johnston My Brother Jack

Student's notes

Student's notes